An Introduction to
MIDDLE ENGLISH

An Introduction
to
MIDDLE ENGLISH

By
E. E. WARDALE, M.A., Ph.D.

LONDON
ROUTLEDGE & KEGAN PAUL LTD
BROADWAY HOUSE: 68-74 CARTER LANE, E.C.4

First published 1937
Second impression 1949
Third impression 1956
Fourth impression 1958
Fifth impression 1962
Sixth impression 1967

Printed in Great Britain by
Compton Printing Ltd
London & Aylesbury

CONTENTS

MAP

ABBREVIATIONS

A.N.	Anglo-Norman.	N.F.	Norman-French.
C.F.	Central French.	O.E.	Old English.
M.E.	Middle English.	O.N.	Old Norse.
N.	Northern.	W.Germ.	West Germanic.

SYMBOLS AND THEIR SOUND VALUES, ETC.

Since Modern English has no pure long vowels, the sound values given here can only be approximate.

ē   pronounced as the first element of the diphthong in **glade**.

ę̄   as the first element of that in **bear**. (Wyld : ę̄).

ō   as in **foe**.

ǭ   as in **saw**.

ā   as in **father**.

y   much as in French **juste**.

ʃ   as the **sh** in **shall**.

tʃ   as the **ch** in **church**.

dž   as the **dg** in **edge**.

χ   as the **ch** in Scotch **loch**.

ȝ   is used here, as a rule, for the spirant, pronounced much as the **y** in **yoke**, but in §§ 12 and 66 it is used for the stop as well, in accordance with O.E. practice.

Following the practice of Luick,[1] Jordan,[2] Wright,[3] and in part, Wyld,[4] the open vowel is indicated by the sign ͕ under it, the long vowel by the line above; ˟ indicates that the vowel may be long or short; an asterisk that the form is hypothetical. A letter enclosed in parentheses indicates that the word occurs sometimes with and sometimes without it, as (i)bounde(n).

[1] *Historische Grammatik der Englischen Sprache.*
[2] *Handbuch der Mittelenglischen Grammatik.*
[3] *An Elementary M.E. Grammar.*
[4] *A Short History of English.*

PREFACE

ONE of the many difficulties in the study of that very intricate subject, Middle English is, I believe, that the beginner is apt to be overwhelmed by the mass of detail he encounters, to be unable, in fact, to see the wood for the trees. My object in this book has been to meet this difficulty in some degree; to emphasize the general character of Middle English; to show its relation to Old English and its position in the whole history of the language, without going more than is necessary into detail. I have tried in short, to show the shape and colour of the wood, only calling attention to individual trees in as far as they are responsible for that shape and colour. Details should be left till later.

Following tradition, I have dealt with Phonology before going on to Accidence, because sound laws, properly understood and applied, should be like pathways leading into the wood and among the trees, they should guide the student from Old to Middle English in the same way. But he is advised to take Chapter III only before attacking the Accidence, and to leave Chapter IV till he has worked through the rest of the book.

My debts to the many writers of Middle English Grammars is, I hope, acknowledged adequately in my references to their books, but to the names of those to whose published works I owe so much must be added that of Professor A. S. Napier, to whose lectures, unfortunately never published, I owe my earliest interest in the history of our language. I should wish, too, to take this opportunity of expressing my great gratitude to Mrs. W. B. Somerset, for her valuable advice in discussing the book at different stages, and for reading the proofs, and to Miss Katherine Harvie for help with the map.

E. E. W.

AN INTRODUCTION TO MIDDLE ENGLISH

CHAPTER I

GENERAL FEATURES OF THE MIDDLE ENGLISH PERIOD

§ 1. The English spoken during what is known as the Middle English period—that is the time between about 1150 and 1450—varied greatly in different parts of the country and a study of the many dialects, all equally important, is so complicated that an introduction may be useful in which those developments only will be considered which are common to all or which, if not universal, are marked characteristics of the areas in which they may be observed.

Before going further it may be well to point out that all linguistic processes being gradual, it is impossible to determine the exact date at which any one development began. Moreover some time must be allowed to elapse before a modification of a familiar sound will be realized sufficiently to be represented in writing ; hence, since our main source of information for Middle English is in the MSS. of the period, any dates given can only be approximate, and the student must be prepared to

1

find slight differences of opinion on these points among those who have treated the subject.

§ 2. But very clear differences are to be observed between the language spoken in England before the Conquest and that of the thirteenth and following centuries, and, since for the study of the whole history of the language, some division into periods is convenient, these differences justify scholars in speaking of a Middle English as opposed to an Old English (Anglo-Saxon) Period.

(a) One of these marked differences is that whereas the latter contained very little foreign element, only a limited number of Latin words and a very few from Celtic and other sources being found, the vocabulary of Middle English has been enormously enriched, especially from Old Norse and French.

(b) Another point of distinction is that whereas in the O.E. period the West Saxon dialect under Ælfred's encouragement of learning had come to be the standard literary dialect, the others being relegated chiefly to colloquial use, in M.E. times no such state of affairs existed. In them all dialects were used for literary purposes and only towards the end of the period do we find that of Chaucer beginning to assume its position as the leading literary language.

(c) But more important than these external points of difference, if perhaps less obvious, and more essential because inherent in the language itself, is the modification which gradually made itself seen in that language. English, like all Germanic tongues, has at all times been governed by what is known as the Germanic accent law, that is by the system of stem accentuation. By this law, except in a few cases, the chief emphasis of the word was thrown on the stem syllable, all others remaining less stressed or entirely unaccented. Thus while in Gothic, of which the records are from two to three hundred years earlier, even long vowels and diphthongs are to be found in inflectional endings, in the earliest O.E. documents only short ones appear in such positions, though all vowels are to be seen in them. Thus a Gothic noun in the nominative plural dagōs is an O.E. daʒas, *days*; a Gothic adjective in the feminine genitive singular blindáizos corresponds to an O.E. blindre, *blind*.

But by the M.E. period we get a further stage. By that time all vowels in unaccented syllables have been levelled under one uniform sound e and O.E. daʒas has become **dawes**; by the end of that period even that e has become mute to some extent in the north, as in Modern English, in which an earlier **dayes** has become **days**. Middle English is thus simply a further stage of Old English in the gradual evolution of the language.

§ 3. The consequences of this levelling of all unaccented vowels under one are twofold.

(*a*) Since many inflectional endings had by this means lost their distinctive value, as when a nominative singular **caru**, *care*, and a nominative plural **cara** both gave a M.E. **care**, or a nominative plural **limu**, *limbs*, and a genitive plural **lima** both gave a M.E. **lime**, those few endings which did remain distinctive, such as the **-es**, of the nominative plural of most masculine nouns, were for convenience' sake gradually taken for general use and the regularly developed plurals **care** and **lime** were replaced by **cares** and **limes**. In the same way and for the same reason the **-es** of genitive singular ending of most masculine and neuter nouns came gradually to be used in other declensions as when for an O.E. **lāre**, *lore's* we find a M.E. **lǫres**.

(*b*) The second consequence follows as naturally. The older method of indicating the relationship between words in a sentence having thus become inadequate, it was necessary to find another, and pronouns, prepositions, and conjunctions came more and more into use. Thus an O.E. **bōca full**, which would have normally given a M.E. **bōke full** was replaced by the phrase **full of bōkes**, and an O.E. subjunctive **hie riden**, which in M.E. would have been indistinguishable from the indicative **riden** from an O.E. **ridon**, by the phrase **if hi riden**. In short, English from having been a synthetic language, became one which was analytic.

§ 4.   But as pointed out in § 1 it is impossible to say

when this change began. The principle of stem accentuation had been working all through the O.E. period and the forms of later O.E. prose, as seen in the works of Ælfric and Wulfstan show a noticeable weakening of the inflectional syllable. Instances are the frequent **-an** for **-um** in the dative plural in Wulfstan, as in **earnungan** for older **earnungum**, *earnings, deserts*, or the nominative plural ending **-e** for the earlier **-a** of feminine adjectives, as in Wulfstan's **lāðe** for **lāða**, *hostile*, or Ælfric's **þēosterfulle wununga** for **þēosterfulla**, *gloomy dwellings*. That the use of " link " words also was becoming more and more common in Old English is to be seen especially in the increasingly frequent appearance of **mid** with the instrumental. Whereas the Wanderer, an early poem, has **hæʒle ʒemenged**, *mingled with hail*, Judith, written in the later half of the tenth century, has the phrase **drencte mid wine**, *plied with wine*.

§ 5. Finally prepositions, pronouns, and conjunctions (link words as we have called them), having become necessary in some cases and therefore introduced into them, a further simplification of the earlier variety of endings was possible, as when the ending **-es** of the nominative plural of the noun was used for all other cases of the plural, or when the nominative singular of the adjective was used for all other cases of the singular as well.

§ 6. The influx of Old Norse and French words must

B

also have begun before the Conquest. A great number of Norse words must have made their way into English as soon as the Scandinavian invaders began to settle in England for the winter months, and still more during the reigns of Danish sovereigns, though few appear in literature till after the Conquest. Their forms, however, when they do appear, make this point certain, as for instance when an Old Norse lāgr appears in Middle English as lǫwe with ā having become ǫ. See § 22, note 1.

A few French words came in, too, before William the Conqueror. Edward the Confessor filled his court with Frenchmen, French monks entered English monasteries, and a certain number of words must have in this way come into the vocabulary of the upper classes.

§ 7. Both these characteristics of the M.E. period, the foreign element in the vocabulary and the modification of the language itself, were thus clearly prepared for in O.E. times and it is not difficult to understand why scholars have varied in the dates they have given as the beginning and end of the M.E. period. 1100–1500 are those most commonly quoted, but perhaps those of 1150–1450 are more satisfactory, with 1050–1150 considered rather as a transitional period during which O.E. characteristics were dying out but those of M.E. were not yet fully established, and 1450 till about 1500 as a similar transition period in which the special features of New English had not yet fully replaced those of M.E. A further division into Early and Late, or Early, Central, and Late M.E., as often made, is too detailed to be considered here.

§ 8. The dialectal divisions of Middle English are naturally based on those of Old English, but their boundaries were modified in some cases, and in consequence of the general tendency of language to break up into diverging groups, it is necessary to divide up some of the larger areas. The great amount of research in Middle English made especially during the last half-century and the increase in the knowledge of the period gained thereby have enabled grammarians to treat the dialects in great detail, but for a preliminary study such as this, it will be more helpful to emphasize the connection with Old English by keeping to general outlines as far as possible.

(1) Thus corresponding to the West Saxon of Old English we get little change in area, but the name South-West is now adopted.

(2) Kentish retains its name, but characteristics of the dialect, already known in O.E. outside it, are now found more widely in regions north and west of the original territory, especially the e for O.E. y, as in merie, *merry*, for O.E. myriȝe. Sometimes the term South-East is found for Kentish, in order to include this wider area.

Note.—West Saxon and Kentish are often classed together as Southern. By others that term is used for West Saxon only, an obviously inadequate designation, since it would seem to imply that Kentish is not a southern dialect. A division of South-West into West and Central South is sound, but not essential at this stage.

(3) The Mercian of the O.E. period must now be divided up into West and East Midland, the dividing line running east of Cheshire, Stafford, Warwick, and Oxfordshire, for by this time the divergence of speech between the inhabitants of the western and eastern parts of the area had become sufficiently pronounced to make this desirable.

(4) The same remark applies to the speech of the inhabitants of North Yorkshire, North Lancashire, and the northern counties of England on the one hand and that of the dwellers in the Lowlands of Scotland on the other, and by, at any rate, the end of the M.E. period it is better to allow for two dialects here also, North English and South Scots.

(5) Lastly, by the end of the M.E. period the language used in London shows such a mixture of forms from East Midland, South-West and Kentish, that it may be said to form a dialect of its own, the London dialect. Thus in place of the four dialects of the O.E. period, we have to allow for six in M.E. or, by the end of the period, for seven.

§ 9. It must, however, always be borne in mind that

the difficulty in giving definite limits in time exists equally for those in space. Geographical boundaries for dialects do not exist ; everywhere there must have been areas in which the recognized characteristics of the regions on either side overlapped, South-West into West Midland, Midland into Northern, and so on. In fact a detailed map should give a finely graded picture in which the characteristics of any dialect merge gradually into those of its neighbour, while they in their turn are gradually absorbed into the next. They should be like the links in a chain ; and in the same way that we took 1050–1150 as an intermediate stage in time, so we have to allow for intermediate areas.

Two such buffer states stand out among the M.E. dialects, and require special notice. The language of the counties of Gloucester, Hereford, and Worcester shows such marked points of resemblance with its neighbour South-West, that it has sometimes been looked upon as an extension of that dialect.[1] It is now, however, more generally considered to be a development of Old Mercian, in which South-Western elements have crept into the West Midland speech. In the same way, the southern parts of Yorkshire and Lancashire and the northern districts of Lincoln and Nottingham

[1] See Morsbach, *Mittelenglische Grammatik*, Einleitung, § 9 ; Wright, *An Elementary Middle English Grammar*, Introduction, § 4, 3.

POSITION OF MIDDLE ENGLISH DIALECTS.

show a similar mixture of character in their dialect, elements from North English and Midland being found side by side.

Both these areas may therefore be taken as showing in a marked degree that gradual merging of one dialect into another, which is to be assumed everywhere, though it may not be so obvious, rather than as possessing distinct dialects of their own.

ORTHOGRAPHY

§ 10. The differences in script between an Old and a Middle English MS. are very striking. Not only have those symbols which have been kept become more pointed in form, but new ones have been introduced to replace older ones or to supply needs which have arisen since the Old English alphabet was fixed. This difference between the MSS. of the two periods is one of the more striking results of the influence of French, to which it is mainly due.

§ 11. The O.E. alphabet had long been inadequate to express the various sounds required of it, many symbols having come to represent two or even more sounds, and when the copying of existing MSS., or the making of new ones came to be chiefly in the hands of Frenchmen, these foreign scribes were naturally more alive to the deficiencies than the former writers who had grown up in the old tradition. They were also better able to supply what was lacking from their familiarity with an alphabet which was more complete, i.e. the French, and with very few exceptions, their innovations were fully justified. All these changes, however, altered greatly the general appearance of the MSS. The details of these changes in orthography will come in better later, in treating of the developments in sound which called for them (Chaps. III, IV). It is enough here to mention the new symbols, or new combinations of old ones whose introduction into the language caused such an alteration in its appearance.

§ 12. The new symbols were **g, k, q, v, w, z**; the fresh combinations were **ch; sh, sch, ss** for O.E. **sc**; and **th**.

g was introduced from French to replace the O.E. **ʒ** symbol when used for the stop, and was sometimes used for the spirant as well. Sometimes it is even found for the spirant **h**. Thus O.E. **ʒōd, ʒrēne, doʒʒa, brinʒan, secʒan, senʒean** were written in M.E. **gōd, grēne, dogge, bringen, seggen, sengen**, and even **seah as sag**. Meanwhile the O.E. **ʒ** lasted on in a modified form, till it was eventually ousted by **y**, which was used in M.E. as consonant and vowel. Thus an O.E. **ʒieldan** would be written in M.E. **ʒelden** and later **yelden**.

§ 13. **k** was not entirely new. It is found, though rarely, in O.E., but in M.E. it came to be written regularly to represent the O.E. **c** before the secondary

vowels ę and i (due to i umlaut), since in those positions
c would have been liable to confusion with the s sound
of the French c before those vowels, as in **cent** and
cinque. Thus an O.E. **cęmpa,** *warrior,* was in M.E.
written **kempe** ; an O.E. **cyning** gave a M.E. **king.**

k was also used for **c** in the combination **cn,** since in
the pointed writing of the time a **cn** would have been
hard to distinguish from an **m.** Thus an O.E. **cnēo,** *knee,*
was written in M.E. **knē.**

§ 14. **q** was an entirely new introduction. It was
used with u to replace the O.E. **cw,** as when an O.E.
cwēn, *queen, woman,* was written **quene.** This was the
one change which was unnecessary, but the French scribes
were no doubt inclined to use their own familiar spellings,
even when they were not helpful.

§ 15. **v** and **z** were borrowed from the French alphabet
to distinguish the voiced **f** and **s** from the voiceless, for
which the old symbols were retained. Thus an O.E.
ʒiefan, seofon, were written in M.E. **given, seven,** and even
in O.E. an occasional example of this **v** may be found.

z was later in being accepted, and was always, as in
modern English, used irregularly. Examples are a plural
ending **-ez** for the older **-as,** to be found in *Sir Gawayne
and the Grene Knight* and other later poems and in
Kentish it appears even initially.

§ 16. The remaining changes in orthography are new
combinations of already existing symbols.

ch was taken from the French to express the (tʃ) sound which had arisen from O.E. ċ initially before palatal vowels and in some other positions, that being the French writing for a similar sound. Thus O.E. ċild, *child*, was in M.E. written child; O.E. ċēosan, *to choose*, became N.E. chesen or chosen; and O.E. wrecca, *exile*, with cc gave M.E. wretche or wrecche.

sh, sch, ss were now used for the O.E. sc, as when O.E. scēawian gave M.E. shēwen, or O.E. sceal was written in M.E. shal, schal or ssal.

§ 17. The combination th was introduced for the older ð and þ. Ð soon died out and the runic þ became less and less used, being, of course, unintelligible to French scribes. Thus an O.E. eorðe, and þæt came to be written in M.E. erthe, and that. The symbol þ lasted on, however, in occasional use till the end of the period, and even survives to the present day in the debased form y in such expressions as *Ye Olde English Shoppe*, in which the y really represents a badly made þ.

§ 18. Lastly the second runic symbol with which the old scribes had been able to eke out their defective alphabet, the Ƿ (wynn) which for some reason is seldom found in editions of O.E. texts, was given up in favour of the writing uu or w, Ƿ being seldom found after 1300. Thus O.E. Ƿæter gave a M.E. water.

§ 19. Vowels show fewer changes. The æ fell out of use probably because the sound was developed to a or e

(§ 51, (1)) and it was no longer needed. The writing of u for O.E. y in those areas in which the sound was retained introduced no new symbol, but merely a difference in usage, as when O.E. **cynn**, kin, was written **cun** in South-West and West Midland.

o was frequently written for u in the neighbourhood of certain consonants, especially **n, m,** and **w,** as when for O.E. **sunu** we find **sone,** or O.E. **wundor** appears as M.E. **wonder.** This is again, however, no introduction of a new symbol, but an adoption of one already existing, made desirable by that same pointed character of M.E. writing which led scribes to use **k** instead of **c** before **n.** See § 13. It is important to realize that no change of sound is indicated.

In later texts **ou** is found for ū, and sometimes **ui** for French ū and O.E. ȳ in those areas in which the latter sound persisted. Thus O.E. **drūpan,** *to droop,* is written **droupen** and O.E. **fȳr,** *fire,* appears as **fuir.** These were no doubt spelling devices used by the scribes to distinguish between the two sound values of M.E. ū [ū and ȳ]. No new symbol was introduced and in the first case, the writing **ou** for ū, no advantage was gained, because M.E. already possessed two slightly differing diphthongs written **ou.**

§ 20. It will be seen that the new symbols which appear in M.E. MSS. are **g, k, q, v, w, z,** and that, as a rule they are purely graphic. In all other cases we have merely a different application of already existing symbols.

Note.—In M.E. **v** and **u** are interchangeable, **u** occurring for the consonant, as in **hauen** *to have*, and **v** for the vowel, as in **vnder** *under*.

VOCABULARY

CHAPTER II

THE FOREIGN ELEMENT IN MIDDLE ENGLISH

(a) OLD NORSE

§ 21. For a full description of the Old Norse and French elements in Middle English, the student is referred to the admirable account in Jespersen's *Growth and Structure of the English Language*, chaps. iv and v, and to those given by Classen [1] and Pearsall Smith.[2] Detailed descriptions of the treatment of individual vowels and consonants will be found in Wright's *An Elementary Middle English Grammar*, chap. v, and, for those who read German, in Luick's *Historische Grammatik der Englischen Sprache*, §§ 381 ff. and §§ 410 ff. All that will be attempted here is to emphasize the general points, those which characterize the influence exercised and provide a setting for the details.

§ 22. The first influx of Old Norse words is undoubtedly to be found some time before the Norman Conquest, and it must have been considerable. This is certain, though the number of words actually recorded in Old English is very small. Among them we have some

---

[1] *History of the English Language.*
[2] *The English Language.*

which are suggestive, for instance, we have laʒu for *law*, griþ for *peace*, dreng for *warrior*, words for law and fighting which are just what the conquerors would have been likely to impose upon the conquered, besides others such as hūsting for *meeting-place*, þræl for *thrall*, hūsbonda for *master of the house*, and so on. That many more came in in spoken Old English, but do not happen to have been recorded, is clear from the forms in which they appear in Middle English, for they have evidently been borrowed in time to fall in with native words and undergo the same treatment of vowels and consonants as they.[1] It is not difficult to see why so few of these O.N. words were recorded in pre-Conquest writings. In the first place, they came in chiefly among a class which produced little literature and, secondly, the greatest number of the Scandinavian settlements through which they would come were in the North and the North and East Midlands, and at that time it was the

---

[1] For instance, O.E. medial and final ʒ became u or i in M.E. according to the nature of the preceding vowel (§§ 59, 66), and an O.E. boʒa, *bow*, became by this process M.E. bowe, and an O.N. laʒu, *law*, recorded as we have seen in O.E., became M.E. lawe. It must be assumed, therefore, that an O.N. lāʒr, *low*, was borrowed also in O.E. since it shows the same treatment of ʒ and was in time for ā to have become ǭ (§ 54). So, too, since an O.N. *vrangr, *crooked*, gave a M.E. wrong, it must have come into the language in time to fall in with an O.E. lang which gave a M.E. long through the stages Late O.E. lāng, M.E. lǭng, long (§§ 72, 73).

West Saxon district in which literature was fostered.
Some of the few that we do find are to be met with
in the later entries in the Anglo-Saxon Chronicle, in
the writings of Wulfstan, archbishop of York, and in
poems such as that commemorating the battle of Maldon
between the English and their Danish invaders.

§ 23. This influence upon the language, though it had
certainly begun before the Conquest, cannot have done
so till some time after those invaders made their first
appearance on English shores. When, as the Chronicle
tells us, three Danish ships appeared off Lindisfarne
in 787, and again when they reappeared, in 793, ravaging
the country, slaying the people, and destroying the
monasteries of Lindisfarne and Jarrow, no effect on the
language would have resulted, nor indeed as long as
raids were made for plunder only. But when in the
ninth century the invaders began to make more perma-
nent settlements, remaining during the winter as the
Chronicle again tells us, first in Thanet in 851 and later
in Northumbria and Mercia, the influx of words would
begin.   Still later, when from 1017 to 1042 a Danish
monarch ruled in England, the intermixture of the
two languages would have become yet greater, and finally
when the two Germanic nations united to oppose the
French invaders, the fusion would have been complete.
Not only would it arise from the daily intercourse of
two peoples living side by side, but there must have

been intermarriages and the children of mixed parentage would naturally be bilingual. Moreover this fusion of the two languages would have been easy because the original differences were not great. The Gunnlaug Saga tells us that the two nations spoke the same language and, though this statement is not quite exact, how little the differences were recognized is clear from the well-known inscription in the churchyard at Aldboro' in Yorkshire, " **Ulf hēt ārǣran cyrice for 'hānum ond Gunware sāule.**" Unless the distinction between the two languages had been little felt and the speaker been practically bilingual, such a mixture of the two, with the O.N. pronoun **hānum** in a sentence otherwise English, would have been impossible. It was just as an Englishman who has lived long in Germany may, when he returns to England, tend to mix German words among his English.

§ 24. This influence of O.N. upon O.E. and M.E. was of a very special character. Both were Germanic languages and the resemblance between the two was, as has been said, very close. While many new words were introduced, such as *leg*, *skin*, *hustings*, in many other cases the same word existed in both languages with only slight differences in vowel or consonant, and the result was merely a modification of existing material. Thus the O.N. vowel was substituted for the O.E. when O.E. **swān**, *peasant*, appeared as M.E. **swein** from O.N.

sveinn; O.E. sweoster, *sister*, as M.E. sister from O.N. systir; or O.E. rǣdan, *to advise*, as M.E. rāthen, rǫthen, from O.N. rāða. In other words it was the O.N. consonant which replaced that of O.E., as when O.E. ȝiefan and ȝietan with the spirant became M.E. given and geten with the stop. Sometimes in a compound word this modification took place in one part only as when the O.N. brūðloup, *wedding*, gave a M.E. brȳdlop, half O.N. and half O.E. in form.[1]

§ 25. The Scandinavians were on the whole at much the same stage of civilization as the English; in the arts of war and shipbuilding and what one may term handicrafts generally they were perhaps in advance of them, as may be seen from the carvings and articles of jewellery they have left, but the cultivation which followed upon the introduction of Christianity and the pursuit of learning in the monastic schools was, of course, wholly lacking to them, since they were still heathen. They could not, therefore, as we shall see later the

[1] Caxton's well-known story of the eggs seems to suggest, however, that certain difficulties lasted on for some time. He tells us how a mercer, named Sheffelde (perhaps because he came from Sheffield, for he was evidently a northerner) went into a house and demanded " **eggys** ". But the " **goode wyf** " answered that she could speak no French. At this the merchant became angry, for he could not speak French either, and things were at a standstill till someone else suggested that what the merchant wanted was " **eyren** ". Caxton ends " **Loo ! what should a man now in thyse days wryte, egges or eyren ?** "

French did, introduce new words for any new ideas in
art or literature which they had themselves brought in.
The Scandinavians mingled among the people and
gradually, with probably little compulsion, but quite
naturally, new words for everyday life crept in from
their speech into English. Instances of such terms are
the modern English *leg* from O.N. **leggr,** and *neck* from
O.N. **hnakki,** for O.E. **scanca** and **heals** ; *knife* from O.N.
knīfr for O.E. **seax** ; *take* from O.N. **taka** for O.E. **niman** ;
window from O.N. **vindauga,** lit. *windeye,* for O.E.
pȳrel ; *root* from O.N. **rōt** for O.E. **wyrt** ; *want* from
the O.N. neuter adjective **vant,** *lacking* for O.E. **wana,**
and many others. Many legal terms also were borrowed,
such as **wǣpnaȝetæce,** *wapentake,* from O.N. **vápnatak,**
and names of different kinds of warships, such as **cnearr,**
a small battleship. Some of these enabled the English
to make finer distinctions than had before been possible,
as, for instance, when the introduction of the O.N. **skinn**
enabled speakers to distinguish between *skin* and *hide,*
O.E. **hȳd,** and that of **reisa,** made possible the differentia-
tion between *to raise* and *to rear,* O.E. **rǣran.** The
introduction of **laȝu** and its use for secular law made
it possible to reserve the O.E. **ǣw** for divine law,
marriage, and some other meanings.

§ 26. Lastly besides bringing in new words and
modifying the form of those already in the language,
O.N. in a few instances changed the meaning of the

native word. For instance O.E. **eorl** meant *a man of good birth*, merely, but its corresponding form in O.N., **jarl**, had gained a special significance and this was passed on to the English word, giving it something of the force of the modern *earl*; O.E. **drēam** meant *noisy revelry*, but the O.N. **draumr** had the meaning of *dream*, which is found in M.E. also; the O.N. **sǫk** had already as one meaning *cause*, while the O.E. force of the corresponding **sacu** was always *strife*, and it may be that the modern sense of *sake* is due to the O.N. or it may have been developed independently in English. Great caution must be used in estimating the influence on meaning exercised by one related language on another, for the same semantic process may have gone on independently in both.[1]

§ 27. From what has been said it will be seen that it is to the familiar words of everyday life that we must look for the O.N. element in the language. Even such little words were taken as the pronoun **they** and the preposition **till** in its ordinary usage, as well as the use of **at** with the infinitive, still heard in the north, but

---

[1] A sentence in the northern poem, the Cursor Mundi, shows how easily the change could have taken place in this particular instance without foreign help. The writer is speaking of the Slaughter of the Innocents, and the sentence there runs, " For Herodes sak, his wiþerwin " *because of (the persecution of) Herod, his foe.* It is just in such a sentence that the earlier, definite meaning of **sacu** could have become obscured in a general sense of " *cause* ", and so have passed on to the modern meaning of " *for the sake of* ".

preserved in standard English only in its shortened form in the word **ado**. With every dialect represented in literature ih Middle English, works from the North and North Midland districts, in which the settlement was most complete, naturally abound in Norse words, but in modern English, with a standard language based on South-East Midland, a large number have been relegated to dialect use only. Outside the ordinary vocabulary O.N. influence is to be seen in many personal names, in place-names in the north, such as those ending in -by and -thorp(e), and in local terms for scenery, such as **Force** for a *waterfall*, and **Gill** or **Ghyll** for a *ravine*. Of O.N. origin is, too, the Yorkshire **Riding**, which is from O.N. **þriðjungr**, *the third part*.

§ 28. The O.N. contributions to the language may be detected by the student of the history of English by the **-sk** in words of Germanic origin, with the exception of **ask, tusk,** and perhaps **flask ;** by the M.E. diphthong **ei** or **ai**, where O.E. had **ā**, as in **nei**, O.E. **nā**, *no* ; the M.E. **ā** where O.E. had **ǣ**, as in **lāta**, O.E. **lǣtan**, *to let* ; the M.E. **ou** or **ō** where O.E. had **ēa**, as in **lōs**, O.E. **lēas**, *loose, free*, **loupen**, O.E. **hlēapan**, *to run*, and by the stop **g** where O.E. had the spirant, as in the examples **give**, **get**, given above, or in M.E. **egg**, O.E. **ǣȝ**, *egg*.

The influence of O.N. is seen chiefly on vocabulary, and on that it was very considerable. At the same time it is not necessary to ascribe every Germanic word not recorded in O.E. but found in M.E. to this source. For instance the verb **to die** is not recorded before the Conquest, but the cognate noun **dēaþ** and adjective **dēad** are common. The verb is quite as easy to develop from an unrecorded Old West Saxon **dīeȝan**, or Anglian **dēȝan** as from the O.N. **deyja**, and it may have been as common in colloquial O.E. as its cognates. But colloquial English has not been preserved ; almost all we have is that in literary usage.

§ 29. Outside the vocabulary O.N. influence is most obvious in its strengthening of the tendency to simplify the inflectional endings. The weakening down of such syllables had been going on, as we have seen, all through the O.E. period and they had in consequence by M.E. times lost much of their earlier importance. The O.N. words which were introduced had often stem syllables so close to those of the native cognates, if not identical with them, that they were easily intelligible, but the inflections differed in the two languages. For instance, the most common O.N. ending for the nominative plural of masculine nouns was **-ar**, while that in O.E. was **-as**, and so on with other classes of words. A tiresome and unnecessary variety of endings was avoided in nouns by taking the general ending **-as**, not only for most O.E. nouns, but for those borrowed from O.N. as well. The spread of these **-as** [M.E. **-es**] plurals became common earlier in the north than in the south, that is, in just those parts in which Scandinavian settlements were most frequent, a fact which strengthens the probability that the process was in some measure helped by their influence. In the case of the adjective this confusing variety may have helped to make speakers concentrate on the stem syllable and gradually drop the endings altogether, though the main cause of their rejection must have been deeper. See § 104. The chief effect, therefore, of O.N. on English grammar has been to hasten the spread of -es plurals to almost all nouns.

§ 30. The influence of O.N. on syntax was very small, and as the points of difference between the two languages were so slight, it is very difficult to decide whether changes to be observed in M.E. are due to native tendencies or to foreign influence. There is, however, one construction in which an existing custom may have been encouraged, and that is in the placing of the preposition at the end of the sentence. This has been a natural tendency in English from pre-Conquest times to the present day, of which an example may be seen in Ælfredian prose, which would not have been affected by Scandinavian influence : " for ðǣm hȳ fōð þā wildan hrānas mid," *for they catch the wild reindeer with (them).* In M.E., however, this usage becomes more common and this may be in part from external influence.

(b) French [1]

§ 31. It has already been said that French words had begun to make their way into English before the Norman Conquest, though not in any great number. Edward the Confessor was half French, his mother being a Norman ; he himself had been brought up to a great extent in Normandy, and when he came to the throne in 1042, he surrounded himself with Frenchmen, to whom he gave high positions at court. They must have introduced many French words into the language of the court, though few have been recorded and there is no evidence that they were adopted generally into the speech of the people. We have, for instance, **capūn**, *fowl*, **sot**, *foolish*, and a few others only. And to French monks who entered English monasteries at this time are no doubt due an example or two of French symbols used for the native ones, as when we sometimes find an occasional **u** for the O.E. **y**, or **v** written for the O.E. medial **f**, as in **given**, O.E. ȝiefen. See §§ 15, 19.

§ 32. The first great influx of French words into the vocabulary was, however, the result of the Norman Conquest, and these penetrated deep into the language. The estates of the English who had opposed William were confiscated and divided among his adherents, and not only were the highest places, civil and ecclesiastical,

---

[1] For fuller accounts of the French element, see § 21.

awarded to the nobles who had supported him, but the
common soldiers, too, had their share of the spoils.
Moreover in the train of the army came numbers of
artisans, tradesmen, and workpeople, who settled in
town and country, and thus the conquerors spread over
the whole of the realm, penetrating into all classes of
society. The result of this conquest was surprising
and entirely different from that of either of those which
had preceded. It did not lead to a driving out of the
speech of the conquered as did the Saxon Conquest,
nor, since the imported language had little affinity
with the native, did it at first produce a modification
of that speech as did the Danish ; the result this time
was the establishment for a while of a second language
in England, the two living on side by side for more than
two centuries. Speaking generally, one may say that
French was spoken at court and by the upper classes,
while English continued to be the speech of the people,
until it later recovered its old position and drove out
French. At the same time there must have been always
and in all classes a certain mingling of the two. The
upper classes must have sometimes needed to get into
direct contact with those beneath them, and the lower
classes, especially those members of them who came
much into touch with the nobles or who wished to better
their own status, must have acquired some amount of
French. There must have been a middle class who were

bilingual, through whom the merging of the two languages was gradually effected

§ 33. The small amount of literature preserved from the time immediately following the Conquest, i.e. from 1066 to about 1200, makes it difficult to trace the rate at which the influence of French made itself felt during that time, but it must have been very slow, for the French words found about that later date are still but few. The Peterborough Chronicle, written soon after 1155, has, it is true, a certain number, but they are such terms as **emperice, justise, prison,** which would have been among the first to be taken over. In the Ormulum, written rather later, about 1200, and rather farther north, in north Lincolnshire, the number of French words is negligible, and the same may be said of the first version of Laȝamon's Brut, or Chronicle, composed in Worcestershire in the first decade of the thirteenth century. In the second text, about fifty years later, there are instances of the native word being replaced by a French one, as when we find in it **pore,** *poor,* for **hǣne,** O.E. **hēanne,** *despised,* in the earlier version.

It was not till the thirteenth century that French superseded English as the second language beside Latin for official use in the Chanceries and Lawcourts, but when once adopted it held its own there and also in the schools till well on into the fourteenth century. In 1362, however, it was determined by **Parliament** (though the determination was not acted upon), that proceedings in the Lawcourts should be in English, the reason given being significant, namely, that French was so little understood, and Trevisa, writing in 1385, tells us that it had then been given up also in the schools. The passage is worth giving here. He is translating Higden's Polichronicon, written in 1353, in which the author regrets the " impairing " of English through the practice, found, he says, in no other country, of obliging children in school to leave their own language and construe their lessons in French, and of teaching gentlemen's children from the time they are rocked in their cradles to speak French. To this Trevisa adds, however, a note of his own since that state of affairs no longer existed. He says "This manner, . . . is some deal changed; for John Cornwall, a master of Grammar, changed the lore in Grammar schools, and construction of French into English, and Richard Pencrich learned this manner of teaching from him, and other men of Pencrich ; so that now, in the year of our Lord a thousand, three hundred, four score and five, and nine of the second king Richard after the Conquest, in all the grammar schools in England children leaveth French and construeth and learneth in English, and haveth thereby advantage on one side and disadvantage on the other ; their advantage is that they learn their grammar in less time than children were wont to do ; disadvantage

is that now children of the grammar schools know no
more French than their left heels, and that is harm
for them and (if) they shall pass the sea and travel
in strange lands and in many other cases also ". In the
same year 1362, which saw the attempt to banish French,
from the Lawcourts, the king opened parliament with
an English speech and finally when in 1399 Henry IV,
a king whose mother tongue was English, came to the
throne, the triumph of that language was complete.
After that French began to disappear in one place
after another, till by the end of the century it was
no longer a living language in England, though it lasted
on in writing, as for instance in legal documents and
in general for the proceedings of parliament till the end
of the fifteenth century.

§ 34. The position of English during these centuries
of French influence is clear from the words of many
writers and may be inferred from many facts. It was
evidently the regular speech of the people. Laȝamon,
at the beginning of the period must have had a public
for his English Brut ; works of general utility, such as
Saints' Lives and the Rule of Nuns were written in
English. But more convincing still are definite statements to be met with, as when we are told in the verse
Chronicle known as Robert of Gloucester's :—

For bote a man conne French me telleth of him lute,
ac [but] lowe men holdeth to Engliss and to here owe
        speche ȝute.

or when the author of the romance, Richard Cœur de Lion, writes :—

> In Frenshe bokes thys rym is wrought,
> Lewed [ignorant] men knowe it nought,
> Among a nundryd [a hundred] unnethes one.

or the writer of the long poem, Cursor Mundi, says :—

> Frankis rimes here I redd,
> comunlik in ilk a sted,
> Mast is it wroght for Frankis man,
> Quat is for him na Frankis can ?
> To laued [ignorant] Inglis man I spell,
> Ðat understandes þat I tell.

These statements make clear the position of French during these centuries. It was the language of the ruling and educated classes, but it does not seem that there was ever any attempt made to drive out English from among the people ; indeed the historian, Ordericus Vitalis, writing between 1130 and 1141, tells us that William himself, at the age of forty-one, made an attempt to learn English, though without apparent success. These facts are important because it has sometimes been affirmed that English was in danger of extermination, whereas it was French that gradually died out as a colloquial language.

§ 35. Meanwhile French had been coming in at different times. As we have seen, the first great influx

was due to the Conquest and the words introduced
at this time would be chiefly from Norman French, a
dialect with an element of Germanic in it, inherited
from the Viking invaders of Normandy, and this, as
modified by English speakers, became what is known as
Anglo-Norman.   The second came from Central or
Parisian French.   From the Conquest onwards the
intercourse between France and England was necessarily
close, the great barons as well as William himself having
property in both realms. Gradually, often as the result
of judicious marriages, the connection with France was
extended to other districts than Normandy. Henry I
married his daughter Matilda to Geoffrey, Count of
Anjou, and when their son, Henry II, came in 1154 to
be king of England, he found himself heir to several
other French provinces, in addition to those which
he had gained by his marriage in 1152 to Eleanor,
duchess of Aquitaine. In these provinces the language
was Central or Parisian not Norman or Northern French.
No great influx of words is to be discerned, however,
in spite of the frequent coming and going between the
two lands, till more than half a century later, when
perhaps the union of all in the effort to resist the tyran-
nical rule of John led to a more complete fusion of the
two languages, and many French words came in.

§ 36. This peaceful penetration of French words was
further helped by literature.   From 1100 onwards

France was the leader in all literary movements in Europe. Not only were French writings well known in England and some works, as for instance the romances Amadas et Ydoine and Ipomedon, actually written there, but many English works were renderings of French matter, and French influence in general was very strong. A certain amount of borrowing from vocabulary, as well as metre and form, was bound to result, and in these ways we get a second great influx of words, those from Central French. Of the two sets of borrowings that from Norman-French is the less numerous, but in one way it may be said to be the more important, because the words penetrated deeper into the language, being carried by the soldiers and their followers among the people. The difference between the two sets may be illustrated from the treatment of the late Latin " captiare ", which was borrowed at both times, first through Norman-French in the form **cacchen**, *to catch*, a verb of universal use, and later through Central French as **chacen**, *to chase*, the word for the sport of the nobles.

§ 37. In general, however, the kind of words borrowed at either period was just what would be expected, they were terms which would be introduced by conquerors at a higher stage of culture and social development, and included words for law, art, literature, music, titles, and the life and habits of the upper classes generally,

while a certain number of war terms was also imposed
by them, though in this department the English had
a rich vocabulary of their own.

A few instances may be sufficient here to illustrate
these borrowings :—

For war we have **armour, battle,** and **war** itself,
but the general term **to fight** is English.

For law there are **court, justice,** and **punish,** but **law**
itself is Old Norse.

Words for art, music, and literature are numerous :
examples are : **art, paint, music, chant, lay, poem,
romance,** and many others, but the simple word **to sing**
is English.

Most titles such as **duke, marquis, baron, marshall**
are French, but the English terms for **king** and **queen,
earl** and **knight** remained ; William had been a duke
only in Normandy, but with the kingdom of England
he took to himself the title of **king** and that of **queen**
for his duchess ; **earl** was kept because it had gained
a special local application from Old Norse ; **knight, too,**
had a special history of its own and therefore remained.

Terms having to do with the lives and customs of
the upper classes are many. Theirs were the **manor**
and the **palace** in contrast to the more homely **cot** and
house ; the **servant** and **butler** of the rich contrast
with the general terms **man** and **maid** ; finally as
Sir Walter Scott has pointed out, the **calf, ox,** and **swine**

of the herdsman's care became **veal**, **beef**, and **pork** on the tables of the nobles.

Note.—For a noticeable exception to this general principle for French borrowings, see § 109.

§ 38. As a result of our borrowings being from two dialects we have a certain number of cases in which the same word has been taken over in two forms. The most obvious of these double borrowings are those with the Norman-French initial **c** beside the Central French form in which that **c** has been developed to **ch**. Examples are N.F. **catel**, *cattle*, beside C.F. **chatel**, *chattel*, both from the Latin **capitale**; N.F. **kenel**, older **kanel**, our *kennel*, *gutter*, beside C.F. **chanel**, *channel*; and the one already given, *catch*, from N.F. beside *chase* from C.F. This may also be the explanation of the modern double forms **ward** and **guard**; **warrant** and **guarantee**; and perhaps **wile** and **guile**. Germanic words with initial **w** when introduced into French kept that **w** in the north, where the influence of the Scandinavian settlers was strong, but developed it to **gu-** elsewhere. In England a N.F. **ward** would fall in with the O.E. **weard** which had the same meaning.

A further set of Norman-French borrowings is to be seen in words with the Anglo-Norman diphthong **au** developed before **n** beside forms with **a** only, as in A.N. **haunche** beside C.F. **hanche**, *haunch*, which explains the modern variable pronunciation; A.N. **haunten**

beside C.F. **hanter,** *to haunt,* and perhaps in **tauni** beside
tanni, our *tawny* and *tan.*

When Chaucer says in the Prologue to the Canter-
bury Tales of the Prioress—

> And Frenssh she spak ful fair and fetisly,
> After the scole of Stratford atte Bowe,
> For Frenssh of Paris was to hore unknowe.

he is probably not, as some think, criticizing her French,
as would be the case now in using the expression French
learnt in England, he is merely saying that she spoke
Anglo-Norman, the French as developed and fully recognized in England.

§ 39. The influence of French on spelling has been
very great and as French symbols were used for native
as well as French words, they have been treated in
another chapter (Chap. I, § 10).

§ 40. The influence on accidence and syntax has been
much slighter. That on accidence is to be seen most
markedly in the strengthening of the already existing
tendency to spread the weak or dental preterite. Already
in O.E. these verbs had been more numerous than the
strong, and the addition of a dental suffix had been
therefore the more usual way of expressing past time.
When in M.E. French verbs were borrowed it would
have been tiresome to take over their various preterite
forms, and a simple way out of the difficulty was to

D

adopt for them the common dental ending of native verbs and to give, for instance, a new preterite **chaunged** to the borrowed French verb, **chaungen**, *to change.* The only exceptions to this process are the verbs **(e)strīven** *to strive* and **cacchen,** *to catch.* The first from its likeness in vowel to the verbs of the first strong class, such as **rīden,** was given an analogical preterite **strōve** on the model of **rōde,** and the second, from its resemblance in form and meaning to the native **lacchen,** *to seize,* was given on the analogy of **lauhte** an irregular weak preterite **caughte** beside a more regular **cacched,** which is also found. French verbs with imperfect tenses in **-iss** frequently carried this suffix through the whole conjugation, as in **punisshen** and **finisshen :** we even find **obeyisshen** for *to obey.*

The result of this treatment of the many French verbs borrowed was to increase the tendency of strong verbs to adopt the weak ending and thus to influence English accidence.[1]

§ 41. No such general influence can be seen on syntax. The chief effect there is in the choice of prepositions to be used to replace the vanishing case endings. Thus **of** was taken to express the genitive because **de** was used in French in that sense ; and when **tō** before the

---

[1] A few adjectives occur in M.E. with the plural ending **-s** of French. Examples are **places delitables, goodes temporeles,** both used by Chaucer.

inflected infinitive, as **tō bindanne**, *for binding*, had lost
its earlier force of indicating purpose and come to be
used with the uninflected infinitive, **for** was adopted in
addition, as in *for to go* on the analogy of the French
use of **pour.** Beyond this French influence on syntax
is only to be traced in a few constructions which occur
in M.E., but have since been given up. Such are the
placing of the definite article before nouns used in a
general sense, as in phrases like " **stille as the ston** "
in which no particular stone is indicated and Chaucer's
" **his byle was blak and as the jet it shon** ", in which
jet is used quite generally, or the placing of " **the** "
before the relative, as in " **the whiche partie is clept
Moretane** ", on the model of the French " **lequel** ".
So too the phrase " **it is me** " is probably due in part
to the French " **c'est moi** ". It may be added here,
that the diphthong **oi**, with one or two exceptions,
indicates a word of French origin, as does the sound
dž (written **g, j**) in the initial position as in **joy, join.**

§ 42. From what has been said it will be clear that
the most striking results of the influence of French
on Middle English are to be seen in the vocabulary
and on spelling. English has at all times kept its own
character in its structure and when its syntax has been
altered, it has been primarily owing to changes within
itself, and not from any foreign impulse, though it
has always been ready to include within its own frame-

work any number of foreign words. English without its French element would be a complete and possible language, but a poor one : the French element without the English foundation would make no complete language.

§ 43. A comparison of the Old Norse and French elements in Middle English is instructive and will help the student to realize the part played by each in the history of the language. It will be seen that they came in first in different parts of the country and that the borrowings are opposed in every way. Speaking generally, it may be said that Old Norse came in first in the north-east and north, French in the south and south-east; Old Norse, a kindred language, modified the existing vocabulary and helped on existing tendencies, French introduced entirely new words ; Old Norse made its way at once into the speech of the people, into the everyday vocabulary; French influenced chiefly the upper classes, giving words for art and literature and " high life " generally ; it enriched the speech of the master, Old Norse, that of the servant.

(c) Low German

§ 44. The Low German element in the M.E. vocabulary has not till recently received much attention. For a fuller account of it the student is referred to § 12 in Jordan's *Handbuch der mittelenglischen Grammatik* and

to Toll's *Niederlandisches Lehngut im Mittelenglischen*.
The small number of words recorded no doubt represents
very inadequately those actually introduced into the
speech of the people, but allowing for this, the con-
tribution of the Low German dialects to the language
must have been very much smaller than that of French
and considerably smaller than that of Old Norse. It
was also different in character. Whereas French influence
is to be seen in every department of the speech of
certain classes, and that of Old Norse penetrated
throughout the vocabulary of certain areas, that of
Low German is chiefly confined to words connected
with certain subjects, i.e. to those having to do with
seafaring—peaceful, or hostile—and with trade and
industry. Like Old Norse, the Low German dialects
were akin to English, " agreeable with it," to use
Camden's expressive phrase, and it might be expected
that their influence would be seen in the same directions,
and that they would not only have introduced new
words, but have also modified existing ones in form or
meaning. It is, however, difficult to find any certain
examples of such modification.

§ 45. Under Low Germans are included here the
Frisians, Dutch, and Flemish, but it is the Frisians and
Flemish whom we find most commonly mentioned,
the term Frisian having been used apparently in Old
English to include all the others, and that of Fleming

in M.E. for the inhabitants of Holland as well as Flanders.

We know that Frisians (Low Germans), had come over with the Angles, Saxons, and Jutes and settled themselves in England in O.E. times.   This is clear from many place-names, such as Dumfries, Frisby, Friston, Friesden, and so on, and from the term Mare Fresicum given to the north part of the Irish Sea.   It is to be assumed also from the mention in the Anglo-Saxon Chronicle of Frisians who fell among the English killed in Ælfred's struggles against the Danes.[1]   Asser speaks of them.[2]   That their skill as sailors was well known is implied when the Chronicler tells us that Ælfred had his ships built neither on the Frisian or Danish model, but just as seemed best to himself. Some slight literary intercourse there must have been too of a primitive kind, for one of the Gnomic verses is concerned with the welcome given by a Frisian wife to her husband returned home from the sea, and some ecclesiastical intercourse, since Ælfred invited the Fleming Grimbald to his court and Dunstan thought out his church reforms at Ghent.

From all this it may be safely inferred that words did creep into the popular vocabulary in pre-Conquest days though not into that of literature.

---

[1] A. S. Chronicle for 897.

[2] Stevenson, *Asser's Life of K. Aelfred*, p. 60.

§ 46. In M.E. times the intercourse between England and the Low Countries was of various kinds. It must be remembered that the queen of William the Conqueror was Matilda of Flanders and Edward the Third's queen was Philippa of Hainault. There were Flemings in the train of the Conqueror, and others who followed for the sake of adventure during his reign and those of his successors, settling in different parts of Britain ; but beyond place-names such as Flenston and Flemingston and the personal name Fleming itself, little trace of these settlers is to be detected in the language, even though the inhabitants of the Peninsula of Gower, "the little England beyond Wales," as Camden tells us it was called, still retain clear signs of their Flemish origin.

§ 47. Far more important in its result on the history of the language was the commercial intercourse between England and Flanders which had existed from the tenth century onwards and the settlements to which it led. This intercourse was first mainly through Flemish sailors who carried away the wool produced in abundance in the great sheep-rearing districts of England and Scotland for manipulation by the skilled weavers of Flanders. Later, however, individual weavers ventured over to England and eventually at the invitation of Edward the Third, no doubt at Philippa's instigation, they came over in their numbers, settling first in London, but later wandering farther afield, especially into Norfolk, where Norwich became in course of time the centre of the wool industry and Worsted gave its name to a particular kind of wool. But the weavers were not alone in their invasion. With them came artisans and craftsmen of all callings—carvers, cordwainers, drapers, glovers, painters, and, especially worthy of mention, goldsmiths and watchmakers, whose skill is still commemorated in the word **clock** which they introduced.

§ 48. As in the case of Norse words, when the foreigners settled down among the English there must have been considerable give and take between two races speaking languages so nearly akin; the words accepted into English would have been largely, though by no means exclusively, those having to do with the occupations in which the Frisians, Dutch, and Flemings possessed the superiority, that is, words dealing with the sea and with industry, but, naturally, coming as these did by way of the people, the bulk of them took time to obtain recognition in literature. Very few appear till after 1300, and there are not many of which we can be certain till the fifteenth century. The bulk of Low German borrowings belongs to modern English. A few instances of words recorded before 1450, may, however, be given.

Under seafaring terms we have **bulwark, lighter, skipper,** and others; terms for weaving and other industries are perhaps **copen**, *to buy*, preserved in " horse coper " ; **frieze** and **holland** (kinds of cloth), **huckster, stripe, spool;** miscellaneous words are : **booze, bung** (of a cask), **cracchen**, *to scratch*, **cant**, *corner*, **dapper, hops, to lack, nag**, and the **clock** already mentioned.

PHONOLOGY

CHAPTER III

A. ISOLATIVE CHANGES

§ 49. The modifications of O.E. vowels which took place in M.E. were some of them isolative, affecting quality only, some of them combinative, affecting quantity chiefly. Of these the changes in quantity are perhaps the more important for the whole history of the language, certainly they are the more complicated and they can be left till later. It is the changes in quality which are treated here and should be studied at this point since they will provide the student with the principles on which to connect up for himself the forms given in the Accidence with those of O.E. with which he is already familiar.

§ 50. O.E. had the following short vowels : a, æ, e, i, ǫ, o, u, y. Of these æ, ǫ, y, only were modified in M.E., the others remaining in sound unless affected by changes in quantity. Thus :—

O.E. abbod, *abbot*, catte gave M.E. abbod, cat.

menn,		helpan	,,	,,		menn,	helpen.
bitter,		biddan	,,	,,		bitter,	bidden.
hlot,		holpen,	,,	,,		lot,	holpen.
guma,	*man*,	sumor,	,,	,,		gume,	sumer.

Note.—It is important to realize that later writings **gome, somer** with **o** for **u** before the nasal are changes in writing only, the sound remaining the same. The **o** occurs before or after **n, m, v, w,** for greater clearness in the MS. Cf. Modern English **come,** and see § 19.

§ 51. The treatment of **æ, ǫ, y,** however, requires notice.

(1) Already in O.E. **æ** had been raised to **e** in Kentish and in some parts of the Midlands. In M.E. **æ** which had remained was retracted to **a,** but the **e** which had arisen from it in Kentish and elsewhere, fell in with original **e** and remained. Thus :—

O.E. **pæþ** gave M.E. **paþ** or **peþ.**

O.E. **wæs** gave M.E. **was** or **wes,** according to dialect.

(2) O.E. **a** before a nasal had been rounded to **ǫ,** but later in West Saxon and Kentish certainly, and probably elsewhere, it went back to **a,** which remained on into M.E. The **ǫ** persisted, however, in the West Midland, as **ǫ,** and is a marked characteristic of that area. Thus :—

O.E. **mann,** earlier **mǫnn,** is general M.E. **mann,** but West Midland **mǫnn.**

O.E. **þank,** earlier **þǫnk,** is general M.E. **þank** or **thank,** but West Midland **þǫnk** or **thǫnk.**

(3) O.E. **y** appears in M.E. in three forms, as **i, e,** and **ü (y).**

Already in O.E. it had been unrounded and lowered to **e** in Kentish and occasional examples of this form are found north and west of that district. In M.E.

this e lasted on, being found in Kentish and outside that area, in Sussex, Essex, and occasionally as far north as Norfolk and South Lincoln. In Northern, East Midland generally, and in three counties of the South-West —Devon, Dorset, and Wilts—it was unrounded to i, although the writing y was still sometimes retained.

In the rest of the South-West, and in West Midland, it remained in sound (y), but the French scribes having much the same vowel in their own language, for which the symbol u was used, adopted that writing for it. Thus :—

O.E. dynt, *dint*, may be in M.E. dint, dent, or dünt, according to area.

O.E. lyft, *left (hand)*, may be in M.E. lift, left, or lüft.

Note.—It must be noted that a y in O.E. has always the ü (y) sound, but in M.E. it is used for that of i, this y being found especially in combination with an n, or m—positions in which in the pointed writing of the M.E. MSS. y was clearer than i.

§ 52. The O.E. long vowels were as follows : ā, ǣ, ē, ī, ō, ū, ȳ. Of these only ā, ǣ, ȳ underwent any modification in M.E. Thus :—

O.E. fēt,	mētan, *to meet*,		
	gave M.E. fēt,		mēten.
rīdan,	tīd,	rīden,	tīd.
gōd,	mōr, *moor*,	gōd,	mōr.
dūn,	drūpan,	dūn, later	drūpen, later
down,	*to droop*,	**doun**,	**droupen**.

§ 53. O.E. ā ǣ, ȳ, were, however, modified.

(1) O.E. ā was rounded to a long, open ǫ sound, something like the modern o in *born*.

Thus O.E. bān, *bone*, is M.E. bǫn ; O.E. māra is M.E. mǫre.

This process was going on during the M.E. period. It appears first in the more southerly East Midland area and spreads gradually westwards and northwards, never getting beyond the Humber till after that period.

(2) The history of ǣ is more complicated, but for general purposes it may be said to have yielded M.E. ē. Thus O.E. hǣlan, *to heal*, is in M.E. hẹlen.

Note (for later use).—O.E. ǣ was of two origins. It might come from a West Germanic ā, and this we may call ǣ[1]. This ǣ is found in West Saxon only ; in the other dialects it had been raised to ē which, falling in with O.E. ē of other sources, remained as we have seen into M.E. and was a long tense ē, something like the vowel in *late*. But the ǣ which had remained in West Saxon was slightly modified in South-West to a long slack ę, something like the sound in the modern *bear*. Thus O.E. slǣpan, *to sleep*, gave M.E. slẹpen in the South-West and slēpen elsewhere.

The other O.E. ǣ (ǣ[2]) was the result of i umlaut on an earlier ā, as in O.E. lǣdan, *to lead*, from lād, *a journey*, or O.E. hǣlan, *to heal*, from hāl, *whole*. This was raised like the other to ē in Kentish, but remained in all the other dialects and gave a M.E. long slack ę as in *bear*, though it was not distinguished in writing from the ē from ǣ[1]. Thus O.E. hǣlan gave a Kentish hēlen, but hẹlen elsewhere. The difference of origin is distinguished in modern spelling, M.E. ē being written chiefly *ee*, and M.E. ę mostly *ea*. This is a point which is of more importance for the later history of the language than for M.E., though accurate rhymers generally kept the two apart.

The following table may make this complicated question clearer :—

O.E. ǣ (W. Germ. ā).	O.E. ǣ (W. Germ. **ai** + **i**).
|	|
M.E. ē (except in West Saxon which has ę̄).	M.E. ę̄ (except in Kentish which has ē).

(3) O.E. ȳ underwent the same threefold treatment as the corresponding short vowel, so that it only remains here to give examples :—

O.E. cȳna (gen. plur.), *cows*, gave M.E. kīne, kēne,
kǖne (ȳ).

hȳdan, *to hide*, gave M.E. hīden, hēden,
hǖden (ȳ).

according to dialect.

§ 54. The history of the O.E. short vowels into M.E. may be summed up in the following table :—

Short Vowels

O.E. a, æ, e, i, ǫ, o, u, y.

M.E. a,　e, i, ǫ, o, u, u (y).

Long Vowels

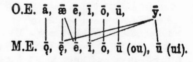

O.E. ā, ǣ ē, ī, ō, ū, ȳ.

M.E. ǭ, ę̄, ē, ī, ō, ū (ou), ū (ui).

DIPHTHONGS

§ 55. Early O.E. had possessed three diphthongs, ea, eo, and ie, all of which could be short or long, but already by the end of that period they had become monophthongs, ea having given æ and ēa, ǣ; eo whether short or long had become œ except, perhaps, in Kentish where it may have gone on to e. ie occurred only in West Saxon. but there it had given i or y by late O.E.

(1) In M.E. æ fell in with early O.E. æ and gave M.E. a or e according to area, § 50 (1).

O.E. ӡeaf, *gave*, is M.E. ӡaf or ӡef. O.E. seah, *saw*, is M.E. sah or seh. O.E̦. ealu, *ale*, is M.E. ale.

(2) O.E. ēa fell in with O.E. ǣ and gave M.E. ę̄; § 53 (2).

O.E. hēafod, *head*, is M.E. hę̄ved. O.E. bēatan, *to beat*, is M.E. bę̄ten.

(3) O.E. œ from eo, short or long, gave in most M.E. areas ĕ short or long according to its origin, but in the South-West and West Midland it remained for some time at the ō̄œ stage written eo, ue, o, u.

O.E. seofon, *seven*, is M.E. sĕven, or seoven; O.E. eorþe, *earth*, is M.E. erþe or urþe. O.E. þēof, *thief*, is M.E. þēf or þēof; O.E. dēor, *wild beast*, is M.E̦. dēr, or dēor.

§ 56. The third O.E. diphthong ī͡e requires more explanation. It is found in West Saxon only, hence its development concerns South-West alone. As has been said, it had become in late O.E. ĭ or y̆, according to its position. This i and y then fell in with the earlier

i and y and had the same development, but being
found in West Saxon only y shows only the South-
West development to ü (y). (See § 51 (3).) In other
dialects O.E. ĭe had corresponded to an ĕ or ĕŏ, M.E. ĕ.
Thus O.E. ȝiefan, *to give*, gave M.E. ȝiven in South-West
but ȝeven elsewhere ; O.E. ȝiest, *guest*, gave M.E. ȝist
in South-West, but ȝest elsewhere; O.E. dīerling, *darling*,
gave M.E. dürling in South-West, but dērling elsewhere.

§ 57. In a certain number of cases, however, O.E.
ĕŏ gave M.E. ŏ with a shift of the accent from the first
to the second element. Thus O.E. ȝeoluca, *yolk*, is M.E.
yolke. O.E. fĕower, *four*, is M.E. foure, and in a few
words ĕa before w shows a similar shift of the accent,
ā then giving a M.E. ǫ, as when O.E. scĕawian, *to look at*,
gave M.E. shǫwen, as well as shęwen, *to show*, with change
of meaning, or O.E. scrĕawa, *shrewmouse*, gave M.E.
shrǫwe, as well as shręwe.

Note.—The writings for these modified forms of the O.E. vowels
did not become fixed at once, and the student must be prepared
for some confusion in the early M.E. texts. For instance, because
O.E. ĕa and ǣ² had come to have the same sound ę, the scribes
frequently confused the original forms and wrote ĕa for O.E. ǣ,
when we find lĕaden for lęden, from O.E. lǣden, *to lead*. In the
same way, O.E. ĕo, ē, and ǣ¹, having all come to the same sound in
M.E., that of ē, the scribes wrote one for the other, as when we find
fĕorde for fērde, O.E. fērde, *he journeyed*, or weoren for O.E.
wǣron, *they were*. Sometimes we even find ĕo for ĕa, as when ĕom
is written for ĕam, *uncle*, though here the sounds were not
identical. See (2) and (3) above.

Formation of New Diphthongs

§ 58. The O.E. diphthongs became, as we have seen, monophthongs in M.E. but their place was taken by new diphthongs which arose, being due to three processes.

(1) The development of a glide i between the front vowels æ, e, and i, and of a glide u between the back vowels, a, o, and u, and a following ȝ, the ȝ being later lost. This process had begun already in O.E.

(2) The development of the same glides i and u before a following h, on the same principle as before ȝ, only that the h was retained, whereas the ȝ was later lost.

(3) The vocalization of w to u after all vowels.

Processes (2) and (3) belong to the M.E. period.

Diphthongization before ȝ

§ 59. Already in late O.E. an i had been developed before ȝ after a front vowel, forming a diphthong with it, and the ȝ continuing to be written for a while, either as the retention of an old spelling, or because it continued to be heard for a time. A form **þeignes**, *thanes*, occurs in the Charters, and others such as **weiȝ**, *way*, **daiȝ**, *day*, are found in the writings of Ælfric. Examples in M.E. are : lai, *lay*, **saide**, *said*, **leide**, *laid*, **weien**, *to move*, *weigh anchor*, for O.E. læȝ, sæȝde, leȝde, weȝan.

A parallel process took place in M.E. before ȝ after back vowels, the u thus produced being usually written **w**.

E

Thus O.E. daʒas, *days*, boʒa, *bow*, gave M.E. dawes, bowe,

Note.—The development of such a glide after i and u necessarily resulted in the lengthening of those vowels. An O.E. stiʒol, *stile*, and fuʒol, *fowl, bird*, gave M.E. stīl, and fūel, written fowel or foul.

§ 60. In the M.E. period i and u glides were developed on the same principle before χ and χt (written h and ht), i after front, and u after back vowels. Examples are :—

M.E. eihte, *eight*, sauh, *saw*, lauhte, *seized*, bouhte, *bought*, for O.E. eahta, later ehta, seah, later sæh, E.M.E. sah,[1] læhte, E.M.E. lahte, and O.E. bohte.

Note.—i and u could only be lengthened by such a process, as in the case of the glide before ʒ. O.E. miht, *might*, gave M.E. mīht, and O.E. þūhte, *methought*, gave M.E. thouhte (ou for ū).

The group eoht appears in M.E. as īht, O.E. reoht, *right*, is M.E. rīht, and O.E. ʒefeoht, *fight*, is M.E. fīht.

§ 61. The vocalization of w also took place in the M.E. period, the u and the w being sometimes written together. This vocalization led to a change in the division of the syllables. Examples are :—

O.E. cla/wu, *claw*, and cnā/wan, *to know*, M.E. clau/e, knǫu/e. O.E. lǣ/we, *lukewarm*, and fēa/we, *few*, M.E. lęu/e, fęu/e. O.E. blō/wan, *to blow*, and sēo/wian, *to sew*,

---

[1] For E.M.E. a for æ, see § 51 (1).

M.E. blōu/en, sēu/en. O.E. scēa/wian, *to look at* or *show*, M.E. shǫu/en, or shēu/en.

Note.—In the examples given above the u has been written to make the actual sound clear, but the writing of the earlier w continued as it does still.

§ 62. Besides the diphthongs thus produced in native words, M.E. has a fair number in words borrowed from French or Old Norse.

From French it has **ai**, as in **lai**, *lay*, **raisin**, *raisin*; **au**, as in **dauncen**, *to dance*, **chaumbre**, *chamber*. This diphthong appears specially in words in which it is followed by **n** or **m** and a consonant.

ei as in **peine**. *pain*, **conveyen**, *to convey*, **feith**, *faith*.

oi, as in **joie**, *joy*, **loiel**, *loyal*, **convoyen**, *to convoy*. This diphthong is chiefly of French origin.

ou in a few words, as in **goute**, *a drop*.

From Old Norse came: **ei** as in **swein**, *swain*, **heil**, *whole*; **ou**, as in **loupen**, *to run*, **goulen**. *to howl*, **nout**, *cattle*.

Note 1.—The constant loss of old and formation of new diphthongs illustrate in a striking manner the life and movement inherent in any spoken language. The O.E. diphthongs disappear, as we have seen, in M.E., and new ones appear; these in their turn are lost in modern English, having given place to new ones, M.E. **bouhte** is modern [bǫt], M.E. **rīdan** is modern [raid].

Note 2.—For all special developments, or developments in special positions, the student is referred to more detailed grammars, such as Wright's *Elementary Middle English Grammar*, or Wyld's *Short History of English*.

CONSONANTS

§ 63. The following paragraphs should be taken in connection with what has been said in §§ 10 ff. of Chapter I, about the new symbols and spellings. There the subject was treated from the point of view of the symbols introduced ; here it is taken from that of the sounds themselves and their history. The actual changes in sound which the O.E. consonants underwent in passing into M.E. were very few, fewer even than those shown by the vowels. Changes in writing were, as we have seen, considerable, but the modifications which they indicate had in most cases taken place at one time or another in O.E.

§ 64. Thus O.E. **f** and **s** had early become voiced between vowels and between a vowel and a voiced consonant, as well as when unaccented. The representation of these voiced sounds by the French symbols **v** and **z** belongs, however, to M.E. and there is also a further development in sound in that later period, in the voicing of **f** to **v** initially in Kentish and South-West, and that of **s** to **z** in Kentish certainly and probably in South-West, though examples are not found there till Modern English.

To the examples therefore already given in § 15, **given, seven,** must now be added M.E. **vīve,** for O.E. **fīfe,** *five,* and M.E. **zingen,** for O.E. **singen,** the latter in Kentish certainly, the former in both Southern dialects.

§ 65. c had at one time in the O.E. period been differentiated to a back (or guttural) and a front (or palatal) stop [c] and [ċ], the latter occurring initially before original front vowels (æ, e, i), usually when doubled, finally after i, and sometimes after -en, the back [c] remaining elsewhere. Before the end of the O.E. period the front [ċ] had probably been developed to the [ʧ] sound of the modern ch. For these two sounds the scribes adopted the writing ch (cch or tch when doubled), that being the writing used in French MSS. for the [ʧ] sound, and they kept the c for the back consonant, except before e and i. Here they wrote k to avoid confusion with French words like cent, cinque, in which the c was pronounced s, and before n for clearness in the MSS. Thus O.E. ċild, cēosan, *to choose*, and wreċċa, *exile*, were written in M.E. child, chēsen, or chōsen, and wrecche or wretche, but O.E. cōl, cann, preserved the old symbol in M.E. cōl, cann, while O.E. cnēo, *knee*, cempa, *warrior*, and cyning, *king*, were written knē, kempe, and king. In O.E., in the combination sc, c had always been a front consonant. In M.E. this sc was developed to [ʃ] written sh, sch, ss, and in the North weakened to s in certain positions.

§ 66. ȝ in O.E. had also stood for more than one sound.

(1) It had early become a back stop before back vowels and consonants.

(2) It remained a back spirant medially and finally after back vowels.

(3) It had become a front stop usually when doubled and sometimes after **en**.

(4) It was a front spirant initially before originally front vowels, medially and finally after them.

By the end of the M.E. period (3) had probably attained the pronunciation of (dž), as in modern English **singe** or written **dg** in **edge**.

In M.E. French scribes introduced their own symbol **g** (**gg** for the O.E. **cg**), some using it for all these sounds, others reserving it for the stops and keeping the O.E. symbol ȝ, and later **y** for the initial spirant (4). O.E. ȝ, however, when medial or final, underwent a modification in M.E., in sound as well as in writing, when the back spirant (2) was vocalized to **u**, which formed a diphthong with the preceding vowel and the front to **i**, forming in the same way a diphthong with the preceding vowel.

Thus O.E. ȝōd, ȝrēne, boȝa, laȝu, secȝan, senȝean, ȝielden, dæȝ, dæȝes, gave in M.E. gōd, grēne, bowe, lawe, seggen (dž), sengen (dž), yelden, dai, daies.

Note.—The writer Orm, in his Ormulum already mentioned, § 33, our earliest spelling reformer, made an attempt to differentiate these four sounds. He distinguished the back stop from the front by placing a long line above it instead of the curl in the right-hand

corner, keeping **g** for the front stop only. The back spirant he
distinguished from the front, by placing an **h** above the old symbol
ʒ which he used for the front. Thus he wrote **seggen**, **laʒͪe**,
and **daʒʒ**, but **gōd** with his new symbol.

§ 67. **h** was lost initially in the groups **hl, hn, hr,**
but remained, though heard less distinctly, before **w.**
Thus O.E. **hnesce,** *tender, soft,* **hlēapan,** *to run,* **hræʒel,**
rail, garment, gave M.E. **nesche, lēpen,** rail; but O.E.
hwæt was M.E. **what,** with inversion of the two consonants, the initial **h** being less clear. When doubled
or final or in the group **ht,** the **h** had a threefold treatment
in M.E. In general in the south it became less and less
clearly pronounced, as indicated by the writings **g, gh,
gt, ght**; in the north the **h** was fully preserved, written
ch as in present-day Scotch, while in other parts of the
country it sometimes passed into **f** as in the present-day
to laugh. Thus O.E. **dohter,** *daughter,* could appear in
O.E. as **dohter, doʒter, dogter, doghter, dochter,** or
dofter, the last rhyming in King Horn with **softe.**

§ 68. O.E. had an interdental spirant which might
be voiceless with the sound of the th in *thin,* or voiced
with that in *worthy,* the latter occurring in the same
positions as the voiced **f** and **v** (see § 64). For these
two sounds the O.E. alphabet possessed the two symbols
þ and **ð,** which were, however, used indifferently by
most scribes. This state of affairs lasted on into M.E.,
with the two sounds kept distinct but the symbols

confused, till both symbols were ousted by the **th** introduced by French scribes, the **ð** disappearing early, the **þ** lasting on longer (see § 17). Thus M.E. **þenchen,** *to think,* with voiceless sound may be found written **ðenchen** and **thenchen,** and M.E. **brōðer,** with voiced sound occurs as **brōþer** and **brōther.** It is probable that in M.E. initial **þ** was voiced in the southern dialects like **f** and **s,** since it is still in South-West, but this obviously cannot be proved from M.E. MSS.

§ 69. **n** fell when final in unaccented syllables and words. O.E. **bindan, ān** gave M.E. **binde, a.** This took place specially before consonants as in **mī bōk** for an older **mīn bōk.**

§ 70. It will be seen that the only consonant changes which were actually made in M.E. were the local voicing of initial **f** and **s,** the vocalization of **ʒ** when medial or final and the treatment of **hw, ht,** and final **h.**

Note.—For the loss of the symbols **ð, þ,** and also of **Ᵽ,** see §§ 17, 18.

CHAPTER IV

B. COMBINATIVE CHANGES

§ 71. From these isolative changes in the quality of vowels we may pass on to those in quantity, which are chiefly combinative, that is due to the position of the vowel, and affecting it in combination with certain consonant-groups or other neighbouring sounds.

In later O.E. and in M.E. a number of lengthenings and shortenings took place, which have materially affected the modern language and therefore need consideration here. They emphasize the gradual development of the language from Old English into and through Middle English, and the difficulty of making a definite division between the two.

I. Lengthenings

§ 72. Already in O.E. short vowels had been lengthened in certain positions. It is possible that this took place at first in the case of all accented vowels when followed by a group of consonants of which the first was a liquid or a nasal, provided that no third consonant came after, for in later O.E. MSS., such as those which contain Ælfric's works, acute accents are found placed not only after vowels undoubtedly long, but occasionally over those before all such groups. We find, for example, the

61

forms ʒelámp, *happened*, éntas, *giants*, as well as bíndan, *to bind*, and bǽrnan, *to burn*.

§ 73. The later history of these vowels shows a gradual tendency to lose their length, and it is probable that the length was given up earlier in the north than in the south and that the process made its way southwards from thence. In any case these lengthened vowels are found in M.E. only before those consonants groups in which the second element is voiced.

Our first source of information is the Ormulum, to the orthography of which reference has already been made more than once. In it the author has worked out for himself a regular spelling system, helped out occasionally by the use of accents, by which he has indicated the length of the vowel followed by two consonants in his time (about 1200) and in his dialect (that of north Lincolnshire). If the vowel is short he has indicated it by doubling the first of the two following consonants ; if it is long he has left the consonant single. Thus he has **hellpenn**, but **bindenn**, that is ĕ but ī.

By this means he has shown that, in his dialect, lengthening was retained before nine groups of consonants only : before -ld, -mb, -nd, -ng, -rd, -rn, -rl, -rð (medial written -rþ), and rz (medial, written rs), provided that no third consonant followed.

Thus we find him writing **alde**, *old* ; **milde** ; **lamb** ; **band**, *bound* ; **stund**, *time* ; ʒ**ung**, *young* ; **corn** ; **eorl** ;

ærd, *kingdom* ; eorþe, *earth.* Before -nd and -ng, however, his usage is not regular, forms such as stanndenn,
ganngenn occurring with nnd, nug, as well as the
examples given above. Other exceptions are not un-
common, some of which may be explained as due to the
influence of related forms, as when we now have *lamb*
instead of the correctly developed *lōmb* from O.E. lāmb,
a new singular having been made from the plural
lambru in which the lengthening was prevented by the r.
In other cases it is difficult to find the necessary related
forms, and the irregularities are best taken as indicating
the beginning of the tendency of the northern forms
to make their way southwards.

§ 74. By the end of the M.E. period the lengthened
forms had disappeared still more, and in the dialect
of Chaucer we find practically only those which have
lasted on to modern times. That is, we have all vowels
long before -ld ; ī and ō (O.E. ā) before -mb ; ī and
ū (written ōu, O.E. ū) before -nd, with a few other
exceptional retentions of older lengthenings. Examples
are : chīld; feeld, *field* ; bȳnden, *to bind* ; lǫmb ; clȳmben,
to climb ; bounden, *bound.*

Chaucer has, however, occasional forms such as soong,
sang ; soond, *sand* ; woord, *word* ; which may be
merely scribal irregularities or may be examples of the
retention of older forms in which the shortening tendency
had not worked.

§ 75. This process has been dwelt upon at some length, because not only is it a curious instance of lengthening pure and simple, with no modification of the liquid or nasal, as in the French nasalization or the modern English pronunciation of words like **port**, but the whole history helps to explain some of the modern irregular spellings, such as that in **mourn, young, bourne**, a doublet of **burn**, *stream*, with the retention in the spelling of the **ou**, the lengthening of O.E. **u** before the **rn** and **ng**. It explains also the spelling with **ea** in **earn, learn, yearn, earl, earth**, this **ea** being the modern writing for a M.E. ę̄ from O.E. **ea** or **eo** lengthened before r + consonant. In these examples we appear to have retained the spelling of the more southerly lengthened forms, but to pronounce the more northerly shortened ones. In **beard**, however, we have preserved the lengthened form as developed in sound in modern English as well as writing.

Note.—For the regular isolative treatment of these vowels see Chapter III.

§ 76. The second period of lengthening took place in Middle English. Between 1200-1250, the short vowels **a, e**, and **o** were lengthened to ā, ę̄, ǭ,[1] respectively in open accented syllables of dissyllabic words;

---

[1] ā, the sound in *calf*; ę, approximately that in *bear*; ē, that in *late*; ǭ, as in *boar*; ō, as in *foe*.

in words of three syllables this did not happen. Examples of these lengthenings are :—

O.E. faran, nama,	M.E. fāren, nāme.
O.E. bĕran, pĕru, *pear*,	M.E. bẹ̄ren, pẹ̄re.
O.E. stolen, hopu,	M.E. stǭlen, hǭpe.

§ 77. The remaining short vowels, the higher ones, i and u, were not lengthened so early or so generally. They were not lengthened till the fourteenth century, and then only in the north and to some extent and rather later in the north Midlands. The i and u, which thus arose, were then lowered to ē and ō respectively. Examples are :—

O.E. bitel, *beetle*, wicu, *week*. M.E. bētel, wēke.
O.E. duru, *door*, wudu, *wood*. M.E. dōre, wōde.

§ 78. Since this lengthening took place in dissyllables only, double forms must have arisen in all words of one or more syllables which were capable of inflection, but, as a rule, one form alone has survived.

For instance an O.E. stæf, plural stafas, must have given a M.E. staf, stāves, and for once both these have been preserved in the modern staff, staves. But in O.E. ȝeoc, *yoke*, plural ȝeocu, M.E. yok yǭkes (with s borrowed from the masculine nouns) the plural form has survived and a new singular yoke made from it. So also in the O.E. ȝeat, *gate*, plural ȝatu, M.E. yat, gātes it is the plural form which has been kept except in a few place-names such as *Simond's Yat*.

On the other hand O.E. pæþ, plural paþas must have given M.E. path, pāthes, but in modern English we have the singular only, with a later lengthening before the th.

§ 79. The same double possibility is found in words of two syllables, as when O.E. bodiʒ, *body*, genitive bodiʒes, gave M.E. bǫdi, bǒdies, with a new nominative later from the genitive, but O.E. æcer, *acre*, genitive æceres gave M.E. āker, äkeres later ākeres from the nominative. Further examples are :—

> O.E. sadol, gen. sadoles, M.E. sādel, sǎdeles, modern English saddle.

> O.E. heofon, gen. heofones, M.E. hę̄ven, hĕvenes, modern English heaven.

> O.E. weder, gen. wederes, M.E. wę̄der, wĕderes, modern English weather.

in which we now pronounce the short vowel of the inflected form, though in heaven and weather we write the long one of the uninflected. But on the other hand in—

> O.E. cradol, gen. cradoles, M.E. crādel, crǎdeles, modern English cradle.

> O.E. beofor, gen. beofores, M.E. bę̄ver, bĕveres, modern English beaver.

we have the long vowel of the uninflected forms driving

out the other. In O.E. **fæder**, gen. **fæderes** ; M.E. **fāder,**
fǎderes, modern *father* (with **th** before the **r** or possibly
from Old Norse), standard English has kept the short,
inflected form in which a persisted through Middle
English and has been later lengthened before the **th**,
but dialects have preserved in *feyther* the uninflected
in which the a has been lengthened, the **ey** repre-
senting the modern development of M.E. ā. In *rather*
beside *reyther* we have another instance of the two
forms being kept.

§ 80. When the second syllable contains a liquid or
a nasal, two explanations are possible. It may be that
the absence of lengthening is due to an early syncope
of the medial vowel. Instances of such syncope are
fairly common, as when we find **fadres, wedres** for
fæderes, wederes. On the other hand the presence of
the two unaccented syllables following would have had
the same effect in M.E. and those words which escaped
the early contraction would still have kept their short
vowels in M.E. before the two unaccented syllables.

It would be interesting if one could see why sometimes
one case and sometimes another has survived. In some
instances one may hazard a guess. In **sadol**, for example,
the dative may have survived because the phrase *in*
the saddle was common then as now ; but with **cradle**
it would have been the accusative which was most
used in expressions like *to rock the cradle*. But this is

of course mere conjecture; we have, unfortunately, too little to judge by.

SHORTENINGS

§ 81. Here again we have to go back to O.E. for the beginning of the earlier shortenings. The general principle is that all long vowels were shortened before any group of consonants, other than one which had caused lengthening. Already in O.E. this shortening had taken place before **ht** and **hs**, and probably before the **pp, tt, kk,** and **dd,** due to doubling before **r**. See *O.E. Gram.*, § 76.[1] Thus an O.E. lēoht, *light*, and þōhte, *thought*, had in O.E. become leoht and þohte, and a nǣddre, *adder*, dēoppra, *deeper*, given **næddre, deoppre.**

§ 82. In M.E. this principle was further developed, and all long vowels were shortened before all groups of consonants, other than the lengthening groups, mentioned previously. It is immaterial how such a consonant group was formed, whether it was original, as in **sōfte**, *soft*, or formed by inflection, as in **lǣdde**, *led*, or by composition, as in **wīsdōm**; the fact of the greater energy required for such a sound group led to the lessening of that spent upon the vowel.

The absence of lengthening before a lengthening group if followed by a third consonant is sometimes taken as due to the M.E. shortenings, but more probably a vowel in such a position was never lengthened.

[1] E. E. Wardale, *An Old English Grammar.*

§ 83. The shortening of long vowels before the two groups -sc and -st requires special explanation. Shortening took place here only if the consonants were in the same syllable ; in dissyllabic forms the syllabic division was made before the s and the vowel therefore remained long, being in an open syllable. Hence again a development of double forms, and an O.E. Crīst, Crīstes, must have given a M.E. Crĭst, but Crī/stes ; an O.E. fȳst, fȳstes, a M.E. fĭst, fī/stes, and an O.E. wȳsc, wȳsce, a M.E. wish, wī/she, where modern English has kept, in the first case, the inflected form with its long vowel and in the others the uninflected in which the vowel was shortened. This special treatment of these two groups is to be explained by the closeness of the sound groups st and sc.

§ 84. Shortening also took place before two unaccented syllables, and here again double forms must have arisen in M.E. ; for example :—

O.E. wǣpen *weapon* gave M.E. wę̄pen, but O.E. wǣpenes was M.E. wĕpenes.

In this case we now pronounce the shortened form, but spell the other.

O.E. hālig, *holy*, gave M.E. hǭli, but O.E. hāligdōm was M.E. hălidom.

O.E. Crīste, dat. sing. gave M.E. Crīste, but O.E. Crīstendōm was M.E. Crĭstendom.

§ 85. Lastly vowels were shortened for want of stress.

Under these are included all those in the second element of compounds and words unaccented in the sentence.

O.E. **biscoprīc** gave M.E. **bishoprĭc**, O.E. **wīsdōm** was M.E. **wĭsdŏm**.

O.E. **ūs**, stressed was M.E. **ous**, but unstressed it gave **ŭs**, the modern form.

§ 86. It will be seen that these lengthenings and shortenings lead to the same results. The positions in which short vowels were lengthened, i.e. before certain groups of consonants and before single medial consonants in words of two syllables, were those in which long vowels retained their length, and those in which long vowels were shortened and short ones remained were the same. We may sum up :—

(1) Lengthening took place before a single medial consonant followed by a single syllable, O.E. **faran** gave M.E. **fāren**.

An originally long vowel retained its length in such a position. O.E. **rīdan** gave M.E. **rīden**.

(2) Before two unaccented syllables a long vowel was shortened. O.E. **hāligdōm** gave M.E. **hălidom**.

A short vowel remained in such a position. O.E. **sădoles**, gave M.E. **sădeles**.

(3) Short vowels were lengthened before certain groups of consonants. O.E. **āld** gave M.E. **āld**, **ǭld**.

Long vowels retained their length before such groups, O.E. **fȳlde**, *defiled*, gave M.E. **fĭlde**.

Note.—Before such groups followed by a third consonant O.E. short vowels were either not lengthened or later shortened. O.E. **lambru** is M.E. **lamber.**

(4) Before other groups of consonants long vowels were shortened, O.E. **mētte** was M.E. **mĕtte**; **lǣdde** was **lădde.**

Before such groups short vowels remained unchanged, O.E. **sĕttan** gave M.E. **setten.**

(5) To these points it may be added that in O.E. short vowels in monosyllables had been lengthened when stressed, as when **hĕ** became **hē.**

In M.E. long vowels in unaccented syllables lost their length, as when O.E. **ān**, *one*, unaccented gave M.E. **ăn.**

Note.—There must have been a tendency to make the stem syllables of equal length either with a long vowel and single consonant or with a short vowel and two consonants, and the lengthening groups must have required little more time or energy than a single consonant.

ACCIDENCE

CHAPTER V

NOUNS AND ADJECTIVES

(a) NOUNS

§ 87. The effect of the weakening of inflections mentioned in Chapter I is to be seen at once in the accidence. The declension of the noun in M.E. is just what must have resulted from it and here again the gradual nature of all linguistic processes is illustrated.

§ 88. Already in O.E. the original ten declensions of the noun had begun to be fused, though the genders continued to be kept apart. Of these ten, three had long been predominant numerically, these being the first or a- class, containing the greater number of the masculine and neuter nouns ; the second, or ō- declension, in which were most of the feminines, and the n- class which had many masculines and feminines and a few neuters.

All other declensions had already by O.E. times dwindled down to what may be looked upon as lists of exceptions. These were, however, very important lists, because of the kind of nouns which they contained, for it is in them that we get many essential words in everyday use, such as those for **father, mother, cow, lamb, oak,** and so on. During the O.E. period the three large classes were, from the frequency of their usage, becoming more and more felt to be the types for the declension of a noun and, in consequence, absorbing the smaller ones into themselves. Thus **-as** had become such a common ending for the plural of masculine nouns that most of those of the third or **i-** declension, such as **cwide,** *speech, saying,* as well as some from the minor declensions, such as **hæleþ,** *hero,* adopted it, making new plurals, **cwidas** and **hæleþas.** Not only had such a word as **fæder,** *father,* taken it regularly, making its plural **fæderas,** but in the north even nouns of the **n-** or weak declension appear with **-as** plurals, though their own ending must have been distinctive enough. We get in the same way feminine nouns of the **i-** class beginning to take to themselves the endings of the larger **ō-** declension, as when **dǣda,** *deeds,* appears for an older **dǣde.**

§ 89. In M.E. this tendency to simplification spread more widely as the endings became weaker, and again it is in the north that the process went furthest and became most general. This simplification of the declension is now to be seen in two ways ; first, in the lessening of the number of classes and secondly, in the lessening of the number of endings for the various cases within the one class.

Taking the number of classes first, we may say that there is only one declension in the North and North Midlands, besides short lists of exceptions, while in the South and South Midlands two classes may be distinguished, those with -es and those with -en plurals, again with lists of exceptions and these rather longer than in the North.

§ 90. Thus the typical declension of a M.E. noun as developed from the O.E. a- declension would be in the North :—

	Sing.		Plur.	
	M.E.	O.E.	M.E.	O.E.
Nom. Acc.	arm, *arm*.	earm.	armes,	earmas.
Gen.	armes,	earmes.	armes,	earma.
Dat.	arm(e),	earme.	armes,	earmum.

Into this nouns from other declensions were gradually absorbed, while in the South there would be a second type :—

	Sing.		Plur.	
	M.E.	O.E.	M.E.	O.E.
Nom. Acc.	hunte, *hunter*.	hunta.	hunten,	huntan.
Gen.	hunte,	huntan.	hunten,	huntena.
Dat.	hunte,	huntan.	hunten,	huntum.

to which the Northern corresponding forms would be **huntes** for the genitive singular and all cases of the plural.

Nouns, however, which had a distinctive plural of their own, such as those with mutation (umlaut), and a certain number of old uninflected plurals preserved their old forms, and thus we get the plurals, **men, fēt, tēþ, folc, childer, shēp, swīn, dēr**, as still in present-day English, besides **dehter, breþer, yeer**, and a few others which have not survived except perhaps in a phrase or two. Already in the Peterborough Chronicle, written a little after 1155 and probably in Peterborough, we get among masculine nouns the forms **sones**, *sons*; **nēves**, *nephews*; **snākes**, *snakes*, for O.E. **suna, nefan, snacan**; among feminines occur **dēdes**, *deeds*; **sinnes**, *sins*, for O.E. **dǣda, synna**, and among neuters are found **werkes**, *works*; **devles**, *devils*, for O.E. **weorc, dēoflu** or **dēoflas**.

§ 91. But in the south while -es plurals were spreading there too, we also get many -en plurals, not only for nouns which had that ending in O.E. but for those also which in O.E. had had the -as ending. Besides plurals like **ēren**, *ears*; **ēȝen**, *eyes*; **fān**, *foes*; **hosen**; **oxen**; **tongen**, *tongues*, in which the original -n has been preserved, we have **sunnen**, *sins*; **glōven**, *gloves*; **spēchen**, *speeches*; **wēden**, *weeds, garments*, for O.E. **synna, glōfa, spǣca**, and **wǣde**.

This method of using -en for a general plural ending was even extended to French words, as in **chainen** for **chaines**.

§ 92. From what has been said it will be seen that not only have we a great simplification in the number of declensions, but that a corresponding simplification has gone on in the number of cases to be distinguished, which brings us to the second point :—

Simplification within the Declension

§ 93. In O.E. four cases have to be distinguished, the nominative, accusative, genitive, and dative, though all declensions do not differentiate all cases. In M.E. as with the generalization of the -es plurals, this reduction of the number of endings for the various cases went on more quickly in the North and North Midlands than in the rest of England. In the long poem, the Ormulum, already mentioned (§§ 33, 73), which is to be dated about 1200 and placed in North Lincolnshire, -es is found in all cases of the plural, as well as for almost all nouns ; and it is thus used also elsewhere. Nouns too, which have other plural endings than -es have the same form throughout the plural. Thus an O.E. **in gōdum þēawum**, dative plural, *in a good manner of life*, has become in M.E. **in gōde þǣwes**, an O.E. **tō ascum**, *to ashes*, is M.E. **tō askes**, or **ashes** ; an O.E. **hī dydon mannum**, *they did to men*, is in M.E. **hī diden men** ; O.E. **bī fōtum** *by the feet*, is M.E. **bī the fēt**. So also with the genitive : An O.E. **biscopa land**, or **abboda land**, *the lands of bishops*, or *abbots* is in M.E. **biscopes land** or **abbodes land**.

From these examples it is obvious why prepositions became more used and the character of the language thereby changed.

§ 94. In the North and North Midlands the change went on so rapidly that only a few instances of old genitive and dative endings are to be found and they are only in expressions like **of alle kinne dēr** (later **alkin**), *beasts of all kinds*, from an O.E. **ealra cynna dēor**, in which the genitive force of **cynna** was hardly felt, and it had almost adjectival significance.

§ 95. In the singular the difference of case endings was preserved to some extent. The **-es** of the genitive singular of masculine and neuter nouns was as distinctive as the **-es** of the plural and, like it, was adopted for nouns of all genders and classes and soon became the recognized ending of that case. Thus an O.E. genitive singular **synne**, *sin's*, or **dǣde**, *deed's*, became in M.E. **sinnes, dedes.**

The **-e** of the dative singular not being so distinctive, did not last on long. To illustrate again from the Ormulum, in that work we find **with Godes helpe** [1]; **to manne**, with the ending still there, side by side with **of þat . . . lac** (*offering*); **of Cristes moder**, with the ending lost, the case being adequately shown by the preposition.

[1] In quoting from the Ormulum, Orm's peculiar spelling has been replaced by normal M.E. forms.

§ 96. In the South and South Midlands, however, the process went on more slowly. The old genitive plural endings -a and -ena lasted on as -e and -ene and even spread and we get such forms as **kingene king**, *king of kings*; **englene bēmen**, *trumpets of the angels*; **fram wȳven pȳne**, *from the women's punishment*; **cnihtene alre fairest**, *fairest of all warriors*, for what would have been in O.E. **cyninga cyning**; **engla** or **englena bīeman**; **wīfa pīne**; **cnihta ealra fægrest**.

Examples of dative plurals surviving are : **over alle blissen**, *above all joys*; **mid deden**, *in deeds*, for O.E. **ofer eallum blissum**; **mid dǣdum**.

§ 97. In the singular also we get examples of old endings lasting on longer than in the more northerly regions. Thus as late as the fourteenth century forms occur in Chaucer such as **cherche dore**; **for his lady grace**; **widwe sone**; for the O.E. **cyrican duru**, *church door*; **for his hlæfdigan miltse**, *for his lady's favour*; **widewan sunu**, *a widow's son*, with old genitives. Compare the modern English **Lady Day**; **Lady Chapel**, for survivals of this southern usage.

The ending also of the dative singular lasted on longer in the South than in the North.

§ 98. To sum up, it may be said that quite early in M.E. in the North and North Midlands -es has become the regular ending for all plurals and all cases of the plural, with a few exceptions which are chiefly those of nouns keeping their old umlauted or uninflected forms. In the genitive singular also -es is the almost universal ending, otherwise the singular was uninflected. In the South and South Midlands, on the other hand, there are two declensions with -es and -en plurals respectively, but as a rule one form was kept for all cases. In the singular -es soon became adopted for the genitive, but many more exceptions or archaic forms are retained. Grammatical gender thus was lost and natural gender alone remained.

For details of the declension of the M.E. noun, the student should consult Wyld and Wright, § 62, note 2.

(b) ADJECTIVES

§ 99. Since the simplification of the noun declension is the result of the weakening of inflections, it would be natural to expect that of the adjective to follow on the same lines. But this is not altogether the case, it will be seen that it has gone much further and soon shows an almost entire loss of inflections.

§ 100. In O.E. the adjective was more highly inflected than the noun, having early borrowed many endings from the pronoun, chiefly in those cases in which the ending of the noun was not distinctive, as for instance in the dative singular, for which the -um of the masculine and neuter as in gōdum, *good*, or the -re of the feminine, as in gōdre, was more definite than the -e of the noun, as in dæȝe, *day*; hofe, *court*; or lāre, *teaching*.

§ 101. But in passing into M.E. nearly all inflection was lost. As with the noun, the process went on earliest and most completely in the North and North Midlands. Already by Orm's time (§ 33, 73) and in his area the strong monosyllabic adjective was undeclined in the singular, and took **e** for all cases of the plural, while those ending in O.E. in **-e** or **-u** had **-e** throughout the singular and plural, and were therefore in fact undeclined.

Weak adjectives in the same way had **-e** throughout the declension, having dropped their final **-n** and weakened the vowels **-a** and **-u** to **-e**.

Dissyllabic adjectives early became uninflected through the loss of the final **-e** in the plural.

Later, when in the fourteenth century final unaccented **-e** became mute, the last trace of inflection died out.

§ 102. The extent of this simplification will be realized if we compare the declension of the adjective in Old and Middle English.

O.E.
Sing.

	masc.	fem.	neuter.
Nom.	heard, *hard*.	heard(u).[1]	heard.
Acc.	heardne.	hearde.	heard.
Gen.	heardes.	heardre.	heardes.
Dat.	heardum.	heardre.	heardum.

[1] **u** early lost after a long syllable.

Plur.

Nom.	hearde.	hearda.	heard(u).[1]
Acc.	hearde.	hearda.	heard(u).[1]
Gen.	heardra.	heardra.	heardra.
Dat.	heardum.	heardum.	heardum.

M E.

Sing.	Plural.
hard.	harde.
grēne (ja stem).	grēne.
narwe, *narrow* [2] (wa stem).	narwe.
þe wīse man.	þe wīse men.
litel.	litel.

§ 103. In the South and South Midlands, though the
final result is the same, the loss went on more gradually.
In the twelfth and thirteenth centuries many traces
of the older forms appear. We get, for instance, phrases
such as a **mīre āgere hand**, *in my own hand*, for an
O.E. **an mīnre āgenre handa**; **ælches weies**, *each way*,
for O.E. **ælces weʒes**; **ænne brǣdne feld**, *a broad field*,
for O.E. **ānne brādne feld**, but other phrases such as
ānne lǣvedi, *a lady*, with a masculine adjective before
an obviously feminine noun, suggest that these endings

[1] u early lost after a long syllable.

[2] w introduced from oblique cases.   O.E. sing **nearu**, plur.
nearwe.

had already lost their significance and were merely formal survivals. They became rarer and rarer during the M.E. period. The most persistent form, and one which is found in the North as well as in the South, is the O.E. ealra, genitive plural of eall, *all*, which survived in the forms aller, alder, alther, as in altherfairest, *fairest of all*, or in Chaucer's oure aller cok, *cock for us all*. A few others occur in compounds such as gōderhēle, *for the good of*, or to wrōtherehēle, *to the injury of*, O.E. tō gōdre- or tō wrāþre hǣle.

Note.—A curious construction may be mentioned here, though it belongs more properly to more detailed accounts. This is the O.E. nānes cynnes, *of no race or kind*, and ǣniges cynnes, *of any race or kind*, which gave the M.E. nōnes kinnes and anies kinnes, and then by wrong subdivision the curious forms noskinnes and anyskynnes. Cf. § 94 for such phrases with cynn.

§ 104. This almost complete loss of inflection in the adjective indicates a change of function. Whereas the adoption of pronominal endings, when they were more definite than those of the noun, must have been in order that the adjective should indicate the relation of the noun to the rest of the sentence (if its own endings failed to do so), in M.E. the sole function of the adjective must have been to express some attribute of the noun, its former one being now taken by the preposition.

Comparison of Adjectives

§ 105. In O.E. the comparative and superlative of adjectives had been formed by the suffixes -ra or -era ; -ost, -ast or -ust, with or without change of vowel (umlaut).

§ 106. In M.E. these suffixes became regularly -re or -ere, later -er and -est. Thus in O.E. glædra, *gladder* ; gladost, gave M.E. gladdre, -er, gladdest ; and O.E. grīettra (*greater*) M.E. grīetest, gave, grettre, -er, grettest, with shortening of the stem vowel. A few adjectives continued to show change of vowel in M.E., as in :—

> lang, lǫng ; lengre, -er ; lengest ;
>
> ōld, eldre, -er ; eldest.
>
> strang, strǫng ; strengre -er ; strengest.

O.E. ȝeonȝ (*young*), ȝienȝra, ȝienȝest gave either :—
(1) ȝung, ȝungre, ȝungest, with the unmutated vowel carried into all forms, or (2) ȝing, ȝingre, ȝingest, with the mutated vowel of the comparative and superlative carried into the positive.

From O.E. forma, *first*, a new comparative former was made in M.E.

§ 107. In O.E. four adjectives good, bad, great, and little formed their comparatives and superlatives from independent stems. These continued into M.E. We find :—

gód ;   bettre -er ;   best.
evil, badde :   werse, wurse (beside badder) ; werst.

muchel, mikel ; mare, mǫre ;   māst,
                                                 mǫst.
litel, lite ;   lesse, lasse ;   lęste

O.E. superlatives in -mest, as innemest, were influenced
by the simple form mǫst and adopted it, giving M.E.
inmōst, ūtmōst, etc.

NUMERALS
Cardinals

§ 108. Of the O.E. cardinal numbers, those for one,
two, three, and eight require comment, the others can
be passed over quickly.

O.E. ān, *one*, gave regularly M.E. ǫn, or ǫ before a
consonant (§ 69). But already in O.E. it had been
shortened to an when unstressed and this an remained
in M.E., giving later a before a consonant. Thus we
get ǫn or ǫ bōk when the particular number is to be
indicated, but a bōk, an erl, where it is no longer felt
to have numerical significance.

O.E. twezen remained on as tweine, tweie, with
occasional genitive and dative forms tweire and twām,
but more commonly twǫ, from the O.E. feminine and
neuter twā, was used for all genders, and as the more
common form, is the one to have survived.

O.E. þrīe, þrēo, gave M.E. þrī, þrē, but here again
as with twezen, the feminine and neuter form þrē,
O.E. þrēo, soon came to be used for the masculine
also. § 55 (3).

O.E. eahta, later ehta or æhta, gave regularly M.E. eiȝte or auȝte, according to dialect. § 55 (1).

Of the other numbers, M.E. foure from O.E. fēower shows a shift of accent from éo to eó. § 57.

O.E. tīene, tēne, gave a shortened form ten beside the regular tēne.

O.E. hund and þūsend, which had been nouns governing a genitive, came in M.E. to be used as numeral adjectives, and hund gradually died out, being replaced by the rival form hundred, from Old Norse.

In the forms of disputed origin hund-seofontig, hund-eahtatig it was dropped, leaving only seventi, eiȝteti.

Ordinals

§ 109. These numerals need very little notice.

In M.E. the n which had been lost by law in O.E. before þ as in seofoðä, niȝoðä, tēoðā, fēowertēoþa was reintroduced from the cardinals, giving a M.E. sevenþe, ninþe, tenþe, fourtenþe.

In parts of England where O.N. influence was strong, the þ was replaced by d giving sevende, ninde, tende, fourtende.

About 1300 the form oþer began to give way to the French secounde. For its original use compare the modern phrase *every other day*.

The O.E. þridda gave a M.E. þirde with metathesis beside þridde,

G

CHAPTER VI

PRONOUNS AND ADVERBS

A. Pronouns

I. PERSONAL

§ 110. The M.E. pronouns are very complicated, and show to some extent only the general tendency to simplification. Most of them being monosyllabic, the usual loss of distinction of case and gender, caused by the weakening of the vowels of unaccented syllables appears only in a case or two ; as a rule distinctions of case are preserved and those of gender in the singular. But on the other hand, pronouns, in any spoken language, are from their very nature, bound to be pronounced with varying degrees of stress, and in consequence to differ in development according to those degrees ; hence arises a complication which is not found in the history of nouns and adjectives. In M.E. monosyllabic pronouns when unstressed in the sentence were treated in the same way as the unstressed syllable in the word, they showed the same weakening of the stem vowel as is seen in that of inflectional endings. Further, in M.E. the multiplicity of forms thus resulting was complicated yet more by dialectal difference of treatment which must be noticed to some extent even in an outline of

M.E. grammar. Here, therefore, a certain number of those most generally met with will be given. They will be found to afford useful tests of dialect.

First Person

§ 111. The O.E. pronouns for the first person were as follows :—

	Sing.	Plural.
Nom.	ic.	wē.
Gen.	mīn.	ūser, ūre.
Dat. Acc.	mē.	ūs.

These gave M.E. :—

	Sing.	Plural.
Nom.	ich, ik, I.	wē.
Gen.	mīn, mī.	ūre, oure.
Dat. Acc.	mē.	ŭs, ous.

Note.—Already in O.E. the earlier accusative **mec** had been replaced by the dative **mē**.

§ 112. In M.E. **mīn, mē, ūre** (later written **oure**) remain and require no further comment, beyond that **mīn, mī** was now used chiefly as the possessive adjective before the noun, as in **mīn bōk**, later **mī bōk**, with loss of **n** before the consonant. **Ic** and **ŭs**, however, illustrate one or other of the points mentioned above and need more consideration.

Ic gave three forms in M.E. In the south it appears as **ich**, the front **ċ** having had its regular development in that area (see § 65). In the north the O.E. form lasted on, but was written **ik**. In the thirteenth century the form **i** is found without the **k**. This loss of **k** is often explained as due to want of stress, but since such a loss of **k** is not found elsewhere, it is probable that it was helped by instances of wrong subdivision, as in phrases like **ic cann**, in which if the accent was on the verb, the first **c** would be lost in the second. This **i** which had thus arisen in the unaccented position was then used in those in which it was accented, and was there lengthened, giving **ī** which has produced the modern form.

Ūs gave two forms, an accented one in which the long vowel was retained and later written **ous**, and an unaccented one in which the vowel was shortened. The latter must have been the one most commonly used, as indeed would be natural in the case of an accusative, since it eventually drove out the accented form and has remained in the modern **us**.

Second Person

§ 113. The O.E. forms for the second person were as follows :—

	Sing.	Plural.
Nom.	þū.	ʒē.
Gen.	þīn.	ēower.
Dat. Acc.	þē.	ēow.

These gave in M.E. :—

	Sing.	Plural.
Nom.	þū, þou.	ȝē, ye.
Gen.	þīn, þī.	eure, oure, youre.
Dat. Acc.	þē.	eu, ou, you.

Note.—As in the case of the first person the old accusative **þec** had been replaced already in O.E. by the dative **þē.**

§ 114. In M.E. only the plural pronouns require comment, those of the singular being regularly preserved in the forms **þū,** later written **þou** or **thou; þīn,** or **þī** before a consonant, later **thīn** or **thī; þē** or **thee.**

In the plural **ȝē** remained as a rule written **ȝē** or **ye,** but by the fourteenth century we find it and the accusative **you** used for the singular in addressing a superior, the so-called plural of respect, which was the beginning of the modern usage.

ēower and **ēow** appear early as **eure** and **oure, eu** or **ou** (§§ 57, 61), and later as **youre** and **you.** The forms with **y** have been explained in two ways. By some it is thought that **éow** became **eów** with shift of accent, and that this rising diphthong then passed through **ió** to **yó,** giving, with the vocalization of the **w,** the modern form *you* (§ 57). A simpler explanation is that the close association in meaning between **yē** and **ēow** led to the initial **y** being carried through the declension. The development of **ēower** followed the same lines as that of **ēow.**

Third Person

§ 115. The history of the third person is much more detailed, the feminine and plural forms in particular needing explanation. The O.E. forms were as follows :—

		Sing.		Plural.
	Masc.	Fem.	Neuter.	All genders.
Nom.	hē.	hēo, hīe.	hit.	hīe, hēo.
Acc.	hine.	hīe.	hit.	hīe, hēo.
Gen.	his.	hiere, heore.	his.	heora.
Dat.	him.	hiere, heore.	him.	hēom.

The M.E. forms were:—

		Sing.	
	Masc.	Fem.	Neuter.
Nom.	hē, a.	hē, hō, schē, schō.	hit, it.
Gen.	his.	hire, here.	his.
Dat. Acc.	him.	hire, here.	hit, it.

Plural

All Genders

Nom.	hī, þey, þai.
Gen.	heore, here, þeire, þaire.
Dat. Acc.	heom, hem, þeim, þaim.

Note.—In these pronouns we have the same process in M.E. in the feminine singular and plural of all genders as in the first and second person in O.E. that is, that the accusative was soon given up in favour of the dative.

§ 116. With the exception of the accusative, the forms of the masculine singular last on, **hē** giving also an unaccented form **a,** but the feminine pronoun requires much comment.

The O.E. **hēo** appears in many forms in M.E. of which **hē** (55 (3)) and **ho** (57) may be taken as representative of the accented development and **ha** of the unaccented. Writings which are found are **heo, he, hi** for the nominative and accusative singular in the South-West; **heo, ho, hue,** in the West Midlands and **hi, ha,** in the South-East. These forms with their initial **h** were retained in the above areas only, where their descendants may be heard to the present day in local speech, but, being liable to confusion with the masculine, in the rest of England they were gradually replaced by **sche, she, scho, sho,** the earliest recorded instance being in the Peterborough Chronicle for the year 1140, where it is written **scæ.** Various views have been propounded on the origin of this form, and of these the most satisfactory is that it comes from the O.E. demonstrative **sīe.**[1]

Already in O.E. in a text known as the Vespasian Psalter, written in the Midland area, the form **síe** occurs for the nominative of the demonstrative instead of the usual **sēo,** and it is used for the personal pronoun as well. If **síe** were pronounced **sié,** with the accent

[1] See Wright, *An Elementary Middle English Grammar*, § 375.

shifted from **i** to **e**, the next stage might have been **sje** [1]
and then **she**. This explanation is satisfactory in that
it gives an O.E. source from much the same locality.
The M.E. spelling need cause no difficulty. O.E. **sc**
had become **sh** (ʃ) in sound, and the older spelling
could quite well have been used for the same M.E.
sound which had come from another origin. [2]

The genitive and dative forms **hire** and **here** are
regular.

The neuter also requires some explanation. In the
nominative and accusative the **h** was early dropped
in the unaccented form, the present-day pronoun **it**
resulting.

The genitive **his** lasted on into the Modern English
period, but early in M.E. the form **it** is found, probably
because **his** was felt to be unsatisfactory, since it made
no distinction between masculine and neuter. **It**, as
genitive, occurs as early as in the Peterborough Chronicle

[1] For a similar development of **sj** to (ʃ), and written **s**, compare
the modern pronunciation of **sure** from French **sûr**, through an
intermediate stage *****sjúr** O.F. **seur**.

[2] Other explanations of the M.E. **she** form are (1) that it is from
a mixture of **hē** from **hēo** and **shō** from **sēo**, with the accent shifted
as above, and (2) that it is due to a wrong subdivision of a northern
phrase such as **bindes hēo**, *she binds*, as **binde shē**. This could,
however, have taken place in the North only, where the ending
of the third person singular of the verb was **s** not **þ**, whereas the
East Midland form given above is much the earliest recorded. See
Lindquist, *Anglia*, 144.

and lasted on till Shakespeare's time. The modern **its,**
formed by simply adding the nominal genitive ending **s**
to nominative of the pronoun, is not found in M.E.
In the neuter instead of the dative replacing the accusative, as in the masculine and feminine, the reverse has
been the case, the accusative having driven out the
dative.

§ 117. The plural forms of O.E. lasted on in the South
and West Midlands for a time as **hi, hy** for the nominative ; **heore, here, hire, hore, hure, hare** for the genitive,
and **heom, hem, hom, ham** for dative and accusative
(§§ 55, 56). In the North and East Midlands, however,
they were gradually replaced by the forms **þei, þey,
thai,** for the nominative ; **þeyre, þaire, thair(e),** for the
genitive and **þeim, thaim,** for the dative and accusative,
from the O.N. **þeir, þeirra þeim.** This was obviously
to avoid confusion between singular and plural. The
first form to be taken in the South was the nominative ;
while Orm, writing in northerly East Midland, has all,
Chaucer, two centuries later, in a very southerly East
Midland area, has the nominative only ; for the oblique
cases he has the regularly developed **here, hem.**

Note.—It illustrates well the closeness of the connection between
the two languages that words of this kind should be borrowed.

§ 118. O.E. had possessed dual forms, **wit, ȝit,** nominative ; **unc, inc,** dative and accusative ; **uncer, incer,**
genitive, for the pronouns of the first and second persons,

and traces of these are to be found occasionally till the end of the thirteenth century. After that they appear to have died out.

Note.—In the South-East Midlands and South-East the forms **hise, is, es,** appear for the accusative plural, **hise** being probably the accented and **is, es** the unaccented developments from **hi** by the addition of the pl. ending **-s** of nouns.

II. REFLEXIVE

§ 119. These may be treated very shortly. Old English had no special reflexive pronoun, the personal pronouns being used in that sense. When, however, they were so used, **self**, either inflected or uninflected, was often added for emphasis. Such pronouns would be in the dative and accusative, as in **mēself, þēself.** In M.E. besides these forms appear **mīself, þīself,** due probably to want of stress, helped by similarity of form with **mī, þī,** O.E. **mīn, þīn.** These later forms seem then to have been interpreted as genitives and **self** looked on as a noun, the construction being extended to the plural, and the forms **oure selven** and youre **selven** appearing. The full acceptance of **self** as a noun with a plural in "**s**" is however not found till the fifteenth century.

III.   DEMONSTRATIVE

§ 120. The simplification of the declension of the demonstrative pronoun was in Middle English even

more drastic than that of the adjective. In O.E. it
had been declined as follows, with distinct forms for
nominative, accusative, genitive, and dative for all
genders in the singular, and for the plural, in which,
however, the genders were not distinguished.

	Masc.	Fem.	Neuter.	All Genders.
Nom.	sē.	sēo.	þæt.	þā.
Acc.	þone.	þā.	þæt.	þā.
Gen.	þæs.	þǣre.	þæs.	þāra, þǣra.
Dat.	þǣm.	þǣre.	þǣm.	þǣm, þām.

It will be seen that all these forms began with þ,
except those for the nominative singular masculine and
feminine. For these the regular M.E. form would have
been se, but the s was soon replaced by the þ of the rest
of the declension, giving þe, later written the, which was
used for the neuter also. Then, as with the adjective,
the inflected forms were given up and the new þe was
used for all genders in the singular. The old neuter
þæt was preserved as that (§ 51), but used to express
emphasis, not gender. The plural þā gave a M.E. þọ̄
(§ 54), which lasted on in occasional use till the end of
the period, giving way eventually to þe. Thus O.E.
sē monn, sēo cwēn, þæt cild, þā cildru became M.E.
þe mann, þe quēne, þe chīld, þō or þe childer.

As with the noun and adjective, this process of simplification went on more slowly in the South than in the North, and many of the old forms were retained there for a time.

Thus in the thirteenth century we get in southern texts þẹre (O.E. þǣre) § 53, 2, for genitive and dative feminine singular ; þan for dative singular, masculine, and neuter and dative plural ; þat still for the simple demonstrative, and as late as the fourteenth century we get þane as accusative singular masculine.

§ 121. O.E. had also a compound demonstrative þēs used for emphasis, and this underwent much the same treatment in M.E. as the above. The inflected forms were early given up except for occasional traces in the South. Those for the nominative had been masculine þēs, feminine þēos, neuter þis, and plural of all genders þās. Of these þis remained as sing. for all genders to express the nearer object ; þēs and þēos gave M.E. þes (§ 55 (3)), from which a þese, these, was formed as plural of þis. The O.E. plural þās gave a M.E. þǭs(e), those, which was used as the plural of þat, that, to express the further object. See above.

Another demonstrative pronoun to be mentioned is ilke, the O.E. se ilca, *the same*. The contracted form with þe occurs in *Chaucer's* þilke bōk, the O.E. se ilca bōc.

IV.   RELATIVE

§ 122. In O.E. the relative connection was expressed
by the particle þe, but þe being indeclinable was
already felt to be inadequate, and was often replaced
by certain locutions to express the different cases. In
M.E. the same difficulty was felt and was met in much
the same way.

(a) The simple relative þe is still found in early
M.E. but side by side with it appears þat, as still
used in Modern English *that*. Thus an O.E. "se monn
þe ic seah" would be in M.E. after the earliest period,
"þe (*the*) man þat (*that*) I saugh".

(b) As in O.E. the demonstrative in the right case
could be used for the relative, so in M.E. another pronoun,
this time an interrogative, could be used. Thus as in
O.E. there might be "se monn þone ic seah", so in
M.E. we find "þe man *which*". Compare *Chaucer's*
"infortunat ascendant *of which* the lord".

(c) As in O.E. demonstrative and relative could be
used together, as in "se monn þone þe ic seah", so in
M.E. we get which and that combined, as in *Chaucer's*
"thilke large bok *which that* men clepe the heven".

(d) As in O.E. the personal pronoun could be placed
after þe or further on in the sentence to indicate the
case, as in an O.E. "se monn þe ic *hine* seah" so in M.E.
we find in the *Man of Law's Tale* "ne was ther Surryen

that he **nas al tohewen**" with the personal pronoun after that.

Finally in M.E. the relative could be omitted even in the nominative, as in "**she beheld a tree was high**".

By the end of the M.E. period the oblique cases of the O.E. interrogative pronoun **hwā**, M.E. **whǭ** (§ 123) could be used as relatives, as in "**this soudanesse** *whǭm* **I thus blame**"; "**Before** *whǭs* **child aungeles synge Osanne**".

The nominative **who** is, however, not used in this way till after the M.E. period. Both **that** and **which** could be used for persons and things without distinction.

Thus while the declension of the adjective and of the demonstrative was soon definitely fixed in its present-day form, and that of the noun was approximating to it, the method of expressing the relative connection remained very fluid, the old difficulties being still felt and the solution of them not yet found.

V. INTERROGATIVE

§ 123. The declension of the O.E. interrogative **hwā** shows a slight simplification. The O.E. forms were :—

	Masc. Fem.	Neuter.
Nom.	hwā.	hwæt.
Acc.	hwone.	hwæt.
Gen.	hwæs.	hwæs.
Dat.	hwǣm, hwām.	hwǣm, hwām.

Hwā gave in M.E. **hwǭ**, later written **who**. § 53 (1).
The accusative, like that of the demonstrative was
given up in favour of the dative and that dative gave
regularly M.E. **hwǭm, whǭm**; but in the genitive the
general principle of simplification is seen when the
ǭ of the other cases was borrowed, giving a **hwǭs,
whǭse**, with one vowel running through all forms,
instead of a regularly developed **hwas**.

VI.   INDEFINITE

§ 124. Only a few of the most characteristic M.E.
forms can be given here. The principal ones are :—

O.E.	M.E.
hwæðer.	hweþer, whether.
āhwæðer.	āwþer, āuþer, *or*.
nāhwæðer.	nāwþer, nōwþer, *neither*.
ǣȝhwæðer.	ǣȝþer, ēiþer.
ǣlc.	ēche, ilk (in North).
ǣnig.	ani, eni.
nān	nān, nōn.
man.	men, me (unstressed).
sum.	sum, som(e).
swilc, swelc.	such(e), swich, swilk (in North).
āwiht, ōwiht.	āuht, āuȝt, āught, ōuht.
nāwiht.	nāuht, nāuȝt, nōuht.

B. Adverbs

§ 125. The treatment of the adverb in M.E. requires little comment. The O.E. ending -līc, -līce, gave a M.E. līke, līche, but was largely replaced by a new ending lī, lȳ from the O.N. -ligr.

CHAPTER VII

VERBS

§ 126. The history of the verb in M.E. is not so straightforward as that of the noun, for while the simplification of form, resulting from the weakening of unaccented vowels went on, the distinction of classes and persons remained and frequent analogical formation introduced further complications. Thus while we have seen that the many earlier declensions of the noun were in M.E. for all practical purposes merged into one, or in the south to two, with lists of exceptions, in the verb we still have strong and weak conjugations to distinguish and, since verbs are classified by their stem or accented syllables, the different classes of strong verbs are still clear. But new complications have arisen, from the borrowing of weak preterite endings by many verbs originally strong, and of forms between the different classes.

§ 127. The personal endings show the regular weakening, but require further explanation as will be seen from the following table :—

		Present	
		O.E.	M.E.
Indic. Sing.	1.	singe.	singe.
	2.	singest.	singes(t).
	3.	singeþ.	singeþ, singes.
Plur. 1–3		singaþ.	singeþ, singen, singes.

H

Present

	O.E.	M.E.
Subj. Sing. 1–3.	singe.	singe.
Plur. 1–3	singen.	singen.
Imperative Sing.	sing.	sing.
Plur.	singaþ.	singeþ, singes.
Infinitive.	singan.	singe(n).
Pres. Part.	singende.	singende, singinde, singing(e), singand.

Preterite

	O.E.	M.E.
Indic. sing. 1.	sang.	sang, sǫng.
2.	sunge.	sunge, sang, sǫng.
3.	sang.	sang, sǫng.
Plur. 1–3	sungon.	sungen, sang(en)
Subj. sing. 1–3.	sunge.	sunge, songe, sange.
Plur. 1–3	sungen,	sungen, songen, sang.
Past Part.	(ʒe)sungen.	(i)sunge(n), sungen.

§ 128. Of the various personal endings the ones which call for comment chiefly are those for the third person singular present indicative, for the three persons of the plural and, less markedly, those for the second singular present indicative, the infinitive, and past participle, the prefix of which also requires a word of explanation. These all afford useful tests of dialect.

(*a*) *2nd Person Sing.*—The general O.E. ending had been -est, which lasted on in most parts, but Old North English (§ 8, 4) had had -es and this persisted in the North in M.E. and is found also in the North Midlands.

(*b*) *3rd Person Sing.*—The general O.E. ending had been -eþ and this like -est survived in M.E. in most parts, but again the Old Northumbrian form -es lasted on in the North and spread into the North Midlands.

(*c*) *Three Persons Plural.*—The O.E. ending -aþ gave regularly M.E. -eþ [later written -eth]. This is found in the two southern dialects and has spread into the south of the West Midlands. In the Midlands generally the ending -en of the subjunctive was substituted for it, to avoid confusion between singular and plural, thus sacrificing distinction of mood for that of number, a change possible as the use of prepositions became more common. In the Northern district the O.E. -as of that area gave -es and this is found also in the north of the Midland district. Thus the ending of the plural present indicative is an obvious test of dialect, and many of these endings illustrate clearly the way in which forms proper to one dialect overflow into the adjacent parts of the next.

(*d*) *Imperative Plural.*—The O.E. form was -aþ which gave M.E. -eþ, -eth, and was kept in the South and even in those Midland areas which took -en for the plural indicative. In the North the O.E. -as was preserved as -es.

(e) *Infinitive.*—The O.E. ending was -an or in the case of some weak verbs -ian. Here the usual tendency to simplify is to be seen in the North and East Midlands where the O.E. -an or North -a was taken as the universal ending, giving M.E. -en or -e. In the South and West Midlands, however, the two were kept apart as -e(n) and -ie(n). Thus an O.E. bodian, *to proclaim*, gave M.E. bode(n) or bodie(n), according to dialect. Further those dialects which kept the -i in the infinitive carried it all through the present. An O.E. bodie, bodast, bodaþ, bodiaþ, gave in those dialects a M.E. bodie, bodiest, bodieþ, bodieþ, and a present participle bodiende. See § 134.

(f) *Present Participle.*—The O.E. ending -ende, lasted on in the South and most of the Midlands, becoming later -inde in the South, and finally -ing(e), by confusion with the verbal noun in -ing, -ung. In the North, however, and North Midlands, the ending -and(e) is found, the rare O.E. -and(e). Thus O.E. singende appears in M.E. as singend, singinde, singinge, singand, according to date and dialect.

(g) *Past Participle.*—The O.E. ending -en was preserved in the North and lost in the South through the stage -e. On the other hand the prefix ȝe- found with many verbs was lost in the North and retained in South in the weakened form -i, though the stage -yi. Thus

O.E. ȝebunden gave in M.E. bounden in the North and ibounde in the South, explaining the two modern forms bound and bounden, or got and forgotten, or the American gotten.

§ 129. Passing on from the personal endings common to all verbs to the separate classes, we have in Middle as in Old English (1) strong verbs, or those which are conjugated by a change of vowel in the stem, and (2) weak verbs, or those which form their past tenses by adding a suffix to the stem of the present; and among the strong verbs we have to distinguish between those in which the change is due to " ablaut " or gradation of the stem vowel, and those in which it is due originally to reduplication.

§ 130. Corresponding to the six classes of " ablaut " verbs in Old English the normal development in M.E. would have been as follows :—

A. Ablaut Verbs

		Pres. Indic.	Pret. Indic. sing.	Pret. Indic. plur.	Past Part.
1.	O.E.	rīde.	rād.	ridon.	(ȝe)riden.
	M.E.	rīde.	rǭd.	riden.	(i)ride(n).
2.	O.E.	lēose, *lose*.	lēas.	luron.	(ȝe)loren.
	M.E.	lēse, lōse.	lę̄s.	luren.	(i)lǭre(n).
3.	O.E.	binde.	band, bond.	bundon.	(ȝe)bunden.
		helpe.	healp.	hulpon.	(ȝe)holpen.
		weorðe, *become.*	wearþ.	wurdon.	(ȝe)worden.

		Pres. Indic.	Pret. Indic. sing.	Pret. Indic. plur.	Past Part.
	M.E.	binde.	band, bǫnd.	bounden.	(i)bounde(n).
		helpe.	halp.	hulpen.	(i)holpe(n).
		wurþe.	warþ.	wurden.	(i)worde(n).
4.	O.E.	bere.	bær.	bǣron.	(ʒe)boren.
	M.E.	bẹ̄re.	bar.	bēren.	(i)bǭre(n).
5.	O.E.	mete.	mæt.	mǣton.	(ʒe)meten.
	M.E.	mẹ̄te.	mat.	mēten.	(i)mẹ̄te(n).
6.	O.E.	fare.	fōr.	fōron.	(ʒe)faren.
	M.E.	fāre.	fōr.	fōren.	(i)fāre(n).

B. Reduplicating Verbs

		Present.	Preterite.	Past. Part.	
1.	O.E.	hāte.	hēt.	(ʒe)hāten.	
		slǣpe.	slēp.	(ʒe)slǣpen.	
		fō.	fēng.	(ʒe)fangen.	
	M.E.	hǭte.	hēt.	(i)hǭte(n).	
		slēpe.	slēp.	(i)slēpe(n).	
		fō.	fēng.	(i)fange(n),	(i)fǫnge(n)
2.	O.E.	fealle.	fēoll.	(ʒe)feallen.	
		blāwe.	blēow.	(ʒe)blāwen.	
		grōwe.	grēow.	(ʒe)grōwen.	
		wēpe.	wēop.	(ʒe)wōpen.	
		bēate.	bēot.	(ʒe)bēaten.	
	M.E.	falle.	fell.	(i)falle(n)	
		blǭwe.	blēw.	(i)blǭwe(n).	
		grōwe.	grēw.	(i)grōwe(n).	
		wēpe.	wēp.	(i)wēpe(n).	
		bẹ̄te.	bēt.	(i)bẹ̄te(n).	

§ 131. While the above are the regularly developed
forms and occur, many irregular forms are also found,
due to analogical formation, owing to wrong associations
in the minds of the speakers. Of these the most common
was to make weak preterites to verbs originally strong,
owing to the fact that the weak verbs were the largest
class and that hence there arose a natural association
of past time with the dental suffix -de or -te of those
verbs. Thus, in the examples just given, for the correct
lẹs, luron, loren we find a pret. loste and past part.
lost; for halp, hulpen, holpen, we get occasionally
helpede, helped; for mat, mēten, meten, we have
metede, meted. For slēp and wēp, weak preterites
slepte, wepte occur already in O.E. and the reason is
not far to seek; it must have been to make a clearer
distinction between present and past in verbs in which
the vowels of the two tenses were so near in sound.

§ 132. A second general tendency to such analogical
formation is seen in the ablaut verbs of Class V, most of
which, owing to the resemblance between their stems
in the present and past, went over into Class IV, and
made their past participles with o instead of e. Thus
we find a past part. troden for treden.

§ 133. The other most noticeable irregular forms are
due to the general tendency to simplification, to do
away with an unnecessary variety of forms.

(1) The O.E. change of vowel in the second and third
persons singular of the present indicative, due to umlaut,

was given up in favour of the vowel of the first singular and the plural, as when O.E. **helpe, hilpest** gave M.E. **helpe helpest**.

(2) There was a tendency to carry one vowel through all the past forms. This might be that of the singular, as when for O.E. **rād, ridon**, we get M.E. **rǭd, rǭde(n)**, or it might be that of the plural, as when for O.E. **bāt, biton** we find M.E. **bit, biten**. The first was more common in the North and the second in the Midlands and South, where, however, the variation of vowel between the first and third person preterite singular and that of the second person singular and the plural is retained in some cases up to Chaucer's time. In the West Midlands especially and chiefly in verbs of the second class, the vowel of the past participle was carried into the preterite plural and thence into the singular, as when for O.E. **cēas, curon, coren**, we get a M.E. **chǭs, chǭsen**.

(3) Corresponding to this tendency to economize on the vowels we get a similar one to carry one consonant through the whole conjugation. For instance the O.E. initial **ȝ** and **c** had been front (palatal) or back (guttural), according to the following vowel and as such had given a M.E. **y** and **ch** or **g** and **c** respectively (§§ 65, 66). But in M.E. one or the other was frequently used for all forms, as when for O.E. **ȝieldan, ȝeald, guldon, golden**,[1] M.E. shows forms with **y** (O.E. **ȝ**) all through

[1] **g** here used for back stop, **ȝ** for front (palatal).

in yēlden, yōlden ; or when O.E .ćēosan, ćēas, curon, coren gave a M.E. chēsen, chę̄s, or chǭs, chǭsen.

(4) The variation of the consonant, due to the working of Verner's Law, was also as a rule given up, as in the above example or when for the regular fōn, *to seize*, we have a new form, fangen, with the consonant of the preterite and past participle in the present.

WEAK VERBS

§ 134. Old English had three conjugations of Weak Verbs, those with preterites in **-de, -ede,** or **-te,** as dēmde, nerede, bohte ; those with preterites in **-ode,** like bodode, and a small class with preterites in **-de,** as in the first class. The normal development of these classes into M.E. would be as in the following table :—

	O.E.	M.E.	O.E.	M.E.
		Present Indicative		
Sing.	1. dēme, *deem.*	dēme.	bodie, *bode.*	bodie, bode.
	2. dēmest.	dēmes(t).	bodast.	bodiest, bodes(t).
	3. dēmeþ.	dēmeþ, dēmes.	bodaþ.	bodieþ, bodes.
Plur. 1–3.	dēmaþ.	dēmeþ, dēmen, dēmes.	bodiaþ.	bodieþ, boden, bodes.
		Subjunctive		
Sing.	dēme.	dēme.	bodie.	bodie, bode.
Plur.	dēmen.	dēmen.	bodien.	bodien, boden.

	O.E.	M.E.	O.E.	M.E.

Imperative

	O.E.	M.E.	O.E.	M.E.
Sing.	dēm.	dēm.	boda.	bodie, bode.
Plur.	dēmaþ.	dēmeþ, -es.	bodiaþ.	bodieþ, bodes.

Infinitive

	dēman.	dēme(n).	bodian.	bodie(n), -e(n).

Present Participle

	dēmende.	dēmende, -inde, -and(e) -ing(e)	bodiende.	bodiende, -ende, -inde, -ing(e), -and(e).

Preterite Indicative

	O.E.	M.E.	O.E.	M.E.
Sing. 1.	dēmde.	dēmde.	bodode.	bodede.
2.	dēmdest.	dēmdes(t).	bododest.	bodedes(t).
3.	dēmde.	dēmde.	bodode.	bodede.
Plur. 1–3.	demdon.	demden.	bododon.	bodedɔ.a.

Preterite Subjunctive

	O.E.	M.E.	O.E.	M.E.
Sing. 1–3.	dēmde.	dēmde.	bodode.	bodede.
Plur. 1–3.	demden.	dēmden.	bododen.	bodeden.

Past Participle

	(ȝe)dēmed.	(i)demed.	(ȝe)bodod.	(i)boded.

	O.E.	M.E.

Present Indicative

Sing.	1.	secge, *say*.	segge, seye.
	2.	saȝast.	seyes(t). § 59.
	3.	saȝaþ.	seyeþ, seyes.
Plur.	1–3.	secȝaþ.	seggeþ, seyen, seyes.

Subjunctive

Sing.	secȝe.	segge, seye.
Plur.	secȝen.	seggen, seyen.

Imperative

Sing.	saȝa.	seye.
Plur.	secȝaþ.	seggeþ, seyeþ, seyes.

Infinitive

	secgan.	segge(n), seye(n).

Present Participle

	secgende.	seggende, -inde, seyende, -and(e).

Preterite Indicative

Sing.	1.	sæȝde.	saide.
	2.	sæȝdest.	saides(t).
	3.	sæȝde.	saide.
Plur.	1–3.	sæȝdon.	saiden.

Preterite Subjunctive

Sing.	1–3.	sæȝde.	saide.
Plur.	1–3.	sæȝden.	saiden.

Past Participle

	(ȝe)sæȝd.	(i)said.

§ 135. In M.E. with the weakening of -ode to -ede, these fell naturally into two classes, those with a medial vowel in the preterite and those in which the suffix was added immediately to the stem. Examples of the two classes are, **bodede**, *boded*, *proclaimed*, beside **dēmde**, *judged*, **bohte**, *bought*, **saide**, *said*. But in weak, as in strong verbs, the regular development was often interfered with by analogical formations, as when for the right form **havde**, O.E. **hæfde**, we get a M.E. **havede** with a medial **e** from verbs like **bodede**.

§ 136. Certain weak and a few strong verbs had in O.E. **bb** or **cȝ** in some forms of the present, but **f** or **ȝ** in the rest of the conjugation. In these in the North and East Midlands the forms with the single consonant drove out the others, but in the South and West Midlands the distinction was long preserved. Thus L.O.E. **secȝan**, *say*, **seȝeþ**, *says*, gave in M.E. in some areas **seien**, **seis**, or **seiþ**, but in the others, **seggen**, **seyeþ** (§ 59).

Note.—For the differences in personal endings, see § 128.

PRETERITE PRESENT VERBS

§ 137. M.E. had the following of these verbs, of which only the forms most generally found are given here :—

(1) **wāt**, **wǭt** ; *I know* ; **wāst**, **wǭst** ; **wāt**, **wǭt** ; plur. **witen**, **wuten**. Infin. **witen**, **wuten**. Pres. part. **witende**, **-inde**, **-inge**, **-and(e)**. Pret. **wiste**, **wuste**. Past. Part. **wist**.

Note.—Forms with **ā** are Northern. § 54 (1).

(2) **ann, ǫnn** ; *I grant* ; plur. **unnen** ; Pret. **ūþe.**

Note.—Analogical forms occur with **u** in the singular, borrowed from the plural.

(3) **can, cǫn** ; *I can* ; **canst** ; **can** ; plur. **cunnen.** Subj. **cunne.** Infin. **cunnen.** Pret. **couþe, coud(e).** Past Part. **couþ.**

Note.—Forms **con, const** with **o** for **a** are found in West Midland. § 51 (2). A singular **cunne** with **u** from the plural also occurs. **Cunnand,** the Northern pres. part., is found as an adjective.

(4) **dar,** *I dare* ; **darst** ; **dar.** Infin. **durren.** Pret. **dorste, durste** with **u** from the Present Plural.

(5) **þarf,** *I need* ; **þarft** ; **þarf** ; plur. **þurven.** Pret. **þorfte, þurfte,** with **u** from the present plural.

(6) **schal,** *I shall* ; **schalt** ; **schal** ; plur. **schulen** or **scholen.** Pret. **scholde** or **schulde,** with **u** from the present.

Note.—Forms **sal, suld** are found in the North. § 65.

(7) **mai, mei,** *I may* ; **miȝt, maȝt, meiȝt** ; **mai, mei** ; plur. **maȝen, mawen, mowen, mai.** Subj. **maȝe, muȝe, muwe** ; § 59. Infin. **muȝen, mowen.** Pres. Part., **maȝend, mowend(e), -inge.** Pret. **miȝte, mihte, mohte, mouȝte, maȝte.**

Note.—**mai** as a plural and **maȝte** are Northern.

(8) mōt, *I must* ; mōst ; mōt. Pret. mōste, muste, mōsten.

(9) āȝ, ōȝ, ōwe, *I own, possess* ; ōwest ; ōwe, ōȝe ; plur. ōȝen, ōwen. Infin. ōwen. Pret. āȝte, auȝte, ouhte. Past Part., āȝen, ǭwen.

Note.—Forms with ā are Northern.   § 53 (1).

§ 138. To these verbs of native origin must be added one borrowed from Old Norse and found in Northern dialects : mun, mon, *I will.* Pret. munde, monde.

ANOMALOUS VERBS

§ 139. (1) bēn, *to be.*

Indic. Pres. : bē, bēst, biþ ; pl. bēn, bēþ.

       or am, art, is ;   ar(e)n, are.

Subj. : bē ; plur. bēn.

Pret. : was, wes ; wēre ; was, wes ; plur. wēren, waren, wǭren.

Note.—Northern has **bēs** all through the present (§ 128), and **was** all through the preterite singular, with **a** instead of **e** in the plural borrowed from the singular. Forms er, ert, es ; pl. ere, es are found in the North, from Old Norse.

§ 140. dōn, *to do.*

Indic. Pres. : dō, dōst, dōþ (N. dōs) ; plur. dōn, dōþ (N. dōs).

Pres. Part. : dōende, -inde, -inge (N. dōand).

Pret. : dide, dede, dude ; plur. diden, deden.

Past. Part. : dōn, ydō(n).

Note.—The forms **dēst, dēþ** occur sometimes in the South, with the mutated vowel retained.

§ 141. **gān, gǭn,** *to go.*

Indic. Pres. : **gō, gōst, gōþ**; plur. **gōn, gōþ.**

Pret. : **yēde, wente.**

Past. Part. : **gān, gǭn, ygǭ(n).**

Note.—North has **gās** all through the present with **ā** retained §§ 128, *a–d* ; 53 (1). The forms **gēst, gēþ,** occur sometimes in the South with retention of the mutated vowel.

§ 142. **willen,** *to will.*

Indic. Pres. : **wille, wolle, welle** ; **wilt, wolt, wult** ; plur. **willen, wellen wollen.**

Pret. : **wilde, wolde** ; plur. **wolden.**

Note.—The **o** in the present singular is from the plural and **i** in the preterite is from the present.

TABLE OF THE MOST STRIKING CHARACTERISTICS OF
EACH DIALECT

	S.W.	S.E.	W.M.	E.M.	North.
Pls. of nouns.	-s, -n.	-s, -n.	-s, -n.	-s.	-s.

Personal Endings of Verbs. Indicative Present.

	S.W.	S.E.	W.M.	E.M.	North.
1st sing.	-e, -ie.	-e, -ie.	-e, -ie.	-e.	-e.
2nd sing.	-est, -iest.	-est, -iest.	-est, -iest.	-est.	-es.
3rd sing.	-eþ, -ieþ.	-eþ, -ieþ.	-eþ, -ieþ, -es.[1]	-eþ, -es.[1]	-es.

[1] Northern forms must always be allowed for in a northern East or West Midland text.

	S.W.	S.E.	W.M.	E.M.	North.
Plur. 1–3.	-eþ, -ieþ.	-eþ, -ieþ.	-en, -i(e)n, -es.[1]	-en, -es.[1]	-es.
Pres. part.	-ende, -inde.	-ende, -inde, -inge.	-ende.	-ende.	-and.

Pronouns

	S.W.	S.E.	W.M.	E.M.	North.
1st sing. nom.	ich, I.[2]	ich, I.	Ich, ic, I.	ic, I.	ic, I.
Fem. sg. nom.	he, hi.[3]	he, hi, ha.	heo, ho, hue.	sche.	scho.
Nom. plur.	he, hi.	he, hi,	he, þei.	þei.	þai, thai.[4]
Acc. plur.		hise, es, is.		es, is.	

Sounds

O.E.	S.W.	S.E.	W.M.	E.M.	North
ā.	ǭ.	ǭ.	ā, ǭ.	ā, ǭ.	ā.
an.	a̧n.	a̧n.	ǫn.	a̧n.	a̧n.
y̆.	ŭ, ĭ.	ĕ.	ŭ.	ĭ.	ĭ.
ǣ[1].	ę̄.	ē.	ē.	ē.	ē.
ǣ[2].	ę̄.	ē.	ę̄.	ę̄.	ę̄.
ō.	ō.	ō.	ō.	ō.	ō, ǖ.

[1] Northern forms must always be allowed for in a northern East or West Midland text.

[2] The I is a later form in all dialects.

[3] Varieties of forms are numerous. Here only those which seem most individual are given.

[4] Earlier texts have þ, later ones th.

INDEX

The numbers given refer to paragraphs. A letter in parentheses thus (I)fange(n) means that the word may occur with or without it.

117